ANSWERS TO QUESTIONS ABOUT THE BIBLE

Robert H. Mounce

BAKER BOOK HOUSE
Grand Rapids, Michigan

Preface

Aristotle said that "philosophy begins with wonder." The desire to know is deeply implanted within the human psyche. James Watt "wondered" about a kettle, Newton about an apple, Archimedes about a bath—and in each case science leaped forward (E. M. Blaiklock).

But science is only one area in which the curiosity of man keeps asking Who? What? Where? When? Why? and How? Man is just as curious about himself and the unseen world as he is about the physical world in which he finds himself. Who am I? Where did I come from? Why do I behave as I do? What lies ahead? How can I find meaning? Perplexing questions such as these have absorbed the intellectual energies of men since the dawn of history. They lie behind the great philosophical systems that shape the contours of human culture.

The Christian faith claims to provide answers for man's essential problems. These answers are found in God's self-revelation in history as recounted in Scripture. Thus the Bible is of great significance for the inquiring believer. In it he learns what God has to say about man's lost condition, what God has done for the redemption of the human race, what is required of man that he may be forgiven of sin, and how man is to live out the inner transformation called the new birth.

For a number of years I have had the privilege of writing a question and answer column for the religious periodical, *Eternity*. Over a period of more than ten years I have studied and thought myself through (or partially through!) a great number of diverse issues that trouble laymen. For my former book, *Answers to Questions That Bug Believers* (Baker, 1977), I collected and reworked about a hundred columns dealing with the Christian and contemporary society. This second book is called *Answers to Questions About the Bible* because it deals with the Bible itself, principles by which the Bible may be correctly interpreted, and answers to apparent contradictions. This book also attempts to explain difficult passages and theological problems, yet it does not claim to be comprehensive. Rather the questions are representative of those kinds of issues which concern the lay readers of Scripture. In the process of answering specific questions I am hopeful that a workable methodology for interpreting Scripture will emerge. Questions yet to be asked are legion. If the book aids the reader in developing a sound approach its value will extend beyond the compass of the immediate questions.

It is important that the reader know that I regard the Bible in its entirety as the written Word of God. Although penned by apostles and prophets, statesmen and poets (to say nothing of farmers and fishermen), its message comes "not at men's word, but as—what it really is—God's word" (I Thess. 2:13, Weymouth). Its interpretation, therefore, calls for the best of scholarship coupled with an intense desire to hear and understand what God Himself has to say.

I am appreciative of *Eternity*'s willingness to allow me to present in a different format material which first appeared there in my column "Here's My Answer." Editors Bill Petersen and Steven Board have always been extremely supportive. My thanks also to Nelda Steen who with her customary efficiency and constant goodwill has typed yet another manuscript.

Contents

1
Interpreting Scripture

This first chapter consists of a number of questions people have raised about the Bible and its interpretation. The questions are specific. Was Jonah actually swallowed by a whale? Did the writers of the New Testament change the sayings of Jesus in order to support their personal views? Why do the experts who can read the original Greek and Hebrew still differ in their interpretations? Does archaeology prove the Bible?

Underlying all these questions is a certain uneasiness which stems from the fact that all written works are subject to interpretation. Who then can guarantee which understanding is correct? Are there some standard rules to be followed by all interpreters, or is each free to make a book mean what he wants it to mean?

We begin with the question most commonly asked about biblical interpretation.

How can I tell if a statement in the Bible is to be taken literally or figuratively?

More than any other problem in biblical interpretation, the question of literal versus figurative continually perplexes both lay interpreter and professional exegete. And like most problems, it arises out of unresolved prior questions. As a partial answer, I would like to set forth some basic interpretive principles which should help clarify the specific issue raised.

First, no one takes all Scripture in a literal fashion. That is, no one takes each word in its basic or denotative sense. Who, upon reading that "the trees of the field shall clap their hands" (Isa. 55:12), would insist upon real applause made by actual hands? Or who honestly expects the returning Christ to have a literal sword protruding from His mouth which He will use to slay the nations (Rev. 19:15)? *Every* interpreter is faced with the problem of deciding between literal and figurative, although many who resist the figurative often leave the impression that for them the problem doesn't exist.

Second, truth may be communicated by figures of speech as well as by straightforward narrative. In fact, in normal conversation we use words in a metaphorical sense far more often than we think. We say, "Toe the mark" or "You've hit the nail on the head" with perfect confidence that others will recognize that we intend our words to be taken in a nonliteral sense. A concept or an idea is not less true if it is communicated by a figure of speech.

Third, it is the responsibility of the interpreter to determine whether the author is using words in their denotative sense or is couching his statement in figurative language. Normally, this is not difficult to discern. In a recipe we understand that two cups of flour means exactly that—*two cups of flour*. But in a poem we would not insist that a girl with a swan-like neck ought to seek employment in a freak show! Effective communication is impossible if the listener is insensitive to the level of discourse he is receiving. To interpret a figure of speech literally is to misinterpret what is being said. In biblical interpretation the tendency toward literalism is often accepted uncritically because the idea of literalness is incorrectly equated with truthfulness.

Here are three familiar passages of Scripture, each of which relies on the believer's instinctual grasp of the nonliteral use of specific words: 1) "The Lord is my shepherd; I shall not want" (Ps. 23:1). 2) "If any one comes to me and does not hate his own father and mother , . . he cannot be my disciple" (Luke 14:26). 3) "If your right eye causes you to sin, pluck it out and throw it away" (Matt. 5:29).

Four suggestions for becoming a better interpreter (which in this context means being more able to distinguish between literal and figurative) are: 1) develop a more sensitive awareness of the various literary genres and modes of communication; 2) desire to let Scripture say exactly what it wishes to say (without undue regard for its implications for your theological position); 3) expand your knowledge of biblical times and customs so that statements and actions are grounded in their original settings, and 4) do not overlook the critical importance of your personal knowledge of God the author.

Quite obviously it is easier to talk theoretically about principles of biblical interpretation than it is to apply those principles to actual passages. Bernard Ramm defines hermeneutics as "the science and art of Biblical interpretation. It is a science in that it is guided by rules within a system, but it is also an art in that the application of the rules is a skill" (*Protestant Biblical Interpretation*, Baker, 1970). Let's turn to a typical question which calls for a judgment about literal versus figurative.

A minister recently said that no intelligent person could accept, in a literal sense, the story of Jonah and the whale. What do you say?

History records many men of intellectual stature who evidently didn't realize how damaging it was to believe in miracles.

If a man is a committed naturalist—that is, if he rules out the supernatural as sustaining any causal relationship within the universe, then it follows quite naturally that Jonah did not stay alive for three days and nights in the belly of some ancient sea monster. It would also follow that Jesus didn't rise from the dead; time always was, and matter is eternal; if there is a God, He has never interfered in the affairs of this world; and everything that has or will happen is theoretically explainable without reference to a higher realm.

Of course, very few of those who reject the possibility of Jonah living inside of a literal sea monster would care to accept the logical implications of their naturalism. But unless they do, their position is inconsistent and therefore unworthy of serious consideration. In my opinion no intelligent person can knowingly commit himself to a logically inconsistent philosophical perspective.

The Christian faith is openly supernaturalistic. It believes not only that God exists, but that He created all things and sustains a continuing relationship with His universe. To accomplish His purposes in time, He "intervenes" in history by causing disturbances, which from man's perspective, are seen as miracles. The same Scripture which presents God in relation to His creation also notes that the mind of man is darkened (Rom. 1:21, 28), and that the whole direction of his life is away from God. Is it any wonder that he boggles at a miracle and does his best to explain it away?

The only situation in Scripture where we should decide against a miracle is when the language is metaphorical and intends a figure of speech rather than a literal interpretation. Isaiah 55:12 speaks of mountains and hills that break forth into singing and of trees that clap their hands—an unusual sing-a-long if we are to take the words at face value! But obviously, we are not.

Some take the entire story of Jonah as an extended metaphor. Jonah is Israel in the belly of the whale (captivity in Babylon) who returns to life (the Restoration) to carry out the will of God. However, I think the words of Jesus, "As Jonah was three days and three nights in the belly of the whale, so will the Son of man be three days and three nights in the heart of the earth" (Matt. 12:40), indicate that the account is to be understood in a literal manner.

To what extent is truth limited to Scripture?

The truth of God and His redemptive activity on behalf of man is limited to divine revelation which now comes to us in the pages of Scripture. If God had not given an explanation, the entire history of the Jewish race and even the life of Christ would be shrouded in mystery.

The full range of truth, however, is not exhausted by revelation. There is truth about the world in which we live (science), truth about ourselves as persons (psychology), truth about the way we organize ourselves in social categories (sociology), etc.

A great number of insights may be gained from secular writers. When Theodore Roszak (a modern exponent of the counterculture) writes that "our actions give voice to our total vision of life," or John Gardner (formerly of Common Cause) notes that if discipline is not internalized in the breast of each free and responsible citizen, we will soon have repressive measures designed to reestablish order, we recognize they are speaking truth. While all truth originates with God, only that truth of supreme importance for man's happiness is guaranteed by divine revelation.

What is a good commentary for a layman interested in studying the Bible on his own?

If you are interested in a commentary that has a high view of Scripture, two one-volume commentaries widely used and well written are *The Wycliffe Bible Encyclopedia* (Moody, 1975) and *The New Bible Commentary* (Inter-Varsity). These are handy references for finding the meaning of a particular phrase or verse.

An indepth study, however, will require more space than a one-volume commentary can afford. As a larger set I recommend the *Tyndale New Testament Commentaries* (Eerdmans, 1957-71) as scholarly, informative, and readable. Remarks on the Greek text are fully understandable to the layman. Among its authors are such prominent names as F. F. Bruce, Leon Morris, and John Stott. A larger and somewhat more technical commentary set is the *New International Commentary on the New Testament* (Eerdmans). Fortunately, the technical discussions are kept to the footnotes so that both layman and professional scholar may benefit from the set. Currently, some of the earlier volumes (from the 1940s) are being replaced and a companion set treating the Old Testament is under way.

We are starting a church library and would appreciate some help in choosing books. What would you recommend?

I hope that every church is compiling a library of select books. Not only is a library an economical method of getting valuable reading material into the hands of the congregation, but it also provides the opportunity for members to share together what they have read. The question allows me to say a few words about what makes a good book and to share the names of some authors who have been of greatest help to me.

It would be difficult to suggest a list of books which ought to be in every church library because churches, like individuals, have special needs and interests. One way to begin a collection of books relevant to the interests and concerns of a specific group is to have each person buy at least one title which has been of significant help to him. This will aid the library committee in starting a collection based on something other than the publishers' recommendations of their own works. Despite what publishers say, not every book is bound to be the greatest contribution to human knowledge since Paul wrote Romans.

A good book must possess two basic ingredients: it must have something to say and say it well. Unfortunately there are fewer good books than one might think. It would be far better to have a select library of good titles than a large library of mediocre volumes.

Now let me venture a list of writers whose books as a whole are nontechnical, possess a broad general appeal, and have been helpful to me. My list is select and reveals personal interests: John Baillie, William Barclay, F. F. Bruce, E. J. Carnell, Reuell Howe, A. M. Hunter, Thomas Kelly, George Ladd, Bruce Larson, C. S. Lewis, Frank Lauback, Keith Miller, J. B. Phillips, Bernard Ramm, Alan Richardson, Charles Shedd, James Stewart, John Stott, Paul Tournier, A. W. Tozer, D. Elton Trueblood, Charles Whiston.

You would also do well to consider other books, not specifically Christian, but helpful for the light they throw on contemporary life. However, these should come by specific recommendation of those within your group who have read them and found them to be helpful.

A number of laymen have asked about books which will help the average person understand the Bible. It is encouraging to see this kind of genuine concern to learn for oneself what Scripture teaches. The number of home Bible studies is constantly increasing throughout America. Some are by design evangelistic, but most reflect the layman's desire to find out for himself what God has to say through the prophets and apostles of old. In an age of instant enlightenment (via the electronic marvels of technological society) people are less and less satisfied with "sitting at the feet" of a Gamaliel or an Apollos.

Books are helpful for general background to Bible study, but there is no substitute for the Bible itself. Scripture is its own best interpreter. Modern speech translations have replaced the archaic phraseology of ancient versions with the vivid idiom of the contemporary world. In my basic New Testament course at Western Kentucky University, the uniform response of young people to the modern translations is unqualified praise.

So take a modern translation and read the Bible as it was intended to be read. Paul's letters are letters, not a collection of unrelated theological and ethical maxims. Read widely. Read the book of Romans in one sitting and see how the theme of righteousness by faith is systematically developed and carried through in all its implications.

My own reading schedule, which takes me through the New Testament every thirty days, involves nine or less chapters a day. Read the entire New Testament three times in the next three months from three different modern translations and you will be amazed at what you have learned *about* the Bible *from* the Bible. Here is the schedule:

(1) Matthew 1-9
(2) Matthew 10-17
(3) Matthew 18-24

21

 (4) Matthew 25-Mark 4
 (5) Mark 5-10
 (6) Mark 11-16
 (7) Luke 1-6
 (8) Luke 7-11
 (9) Luke 12-18
(10) Luke 19-24
(11) John 1-7
(12) John 8-14
(13) John 15-21
(14) Acts 1-7
(15) Acts 8-14
(16) Acts 15-20
(17) Acts 21-28
(18) Romans 1-6
(19) Romans 7-16
(20) I Corinthians 1-9
(21) I Corinthians 10-16
(22) II Corinthians
(23) Galatians, Ephesians
(24) Philippians, Colossians, I Thessalonians
(25) II Thessalonians, I and II Timothy
(26) Titus, Philemon, Hebrews 1-9
(27) Hebrews 10-13, James
(28) I and II Peter, I, II, and III John
(29) Jude, Revelation 1-11
(30) Revelation 12-22

My suggestion would be to copy this schedule onto the flyleaf of your Bible or onto a card which you can keep in your Bible for handy reference.

One further suggestion: If you miss a day,

don't try to make up the reading before you go ahead. Read the portion that corresponds with the day of the month and then when you have time, go back and read what you missed. Whatever you do, don't make Bible reading a chore!

The question of the uniqueness of Scripture occasionally arises. Did the writers of the Bible utilize sources or did all they wrote come directly from God? This is the general question which lies behind the following specific inquiry.

I have recently read that the Hebrews borrowed the best Canaanite literature and incorporated it into the Old Testament. If this is so, in which portions can it be found?

The background for this question has to do with the excavations at Ras Shamra on the Syrian coast. Among the many materials uncovered there since 1929 were more than 350 Ugaritic texts. Included are a number of epics written in cuneiform on a series of tablets. These have become important sources for knowledge of Canaanite religion and mythology.

They introduce us to the antics of the storm god, Baal (controller of rain and fertility), his consort, Anat (goddess of war, love, and fertility), King Keret, Lady Asherah "of the Sea," and others. The texts amply demonstrate the exceedingly base nature of Canaanitish worship and its degrading effect upon the social life of the area.

In spite of the totally different moral and religious atmosphere of the Ugaritic materials, they do exhibit some incidental similarities to the Old Testament. For example, the terminology of the ritual system is not unlike that of Leviticus with its burnt, trespass, and peace offerings. The syntax and poetic structure of the Ugaritic hymns remind us of the Song of Miriam (Exod. 15) and certain of the Psalms (e. g., 29 and 58). Many expressions occurring in the poetic sections of the Old Testament are also paralleled in the Ugaritic texts.

These verbal similarities do not, of course, argue for a Canaanite source for Old Testament revelation. What they do demonstrate is that the Old Testament was written from within a cultural milieu that was to some extent shared with Israel's neighbors. To read the Ras Shamra epics with their emphasis on war, sensuous love, and sacred prostitution is to realize that whatever verbal similarities may exist, the whole spirit and practice of Israelitish worship was radically different.

Is there any evidence outside the New Testament that there ever was an historical Jesus?

In a work produced in 1877, the German theologian and biblical critic, Bruno Bauer, concluded that the person Jesus has never existed. He was only an imaginary being—a combination of Seneca (a Roman philosopher) and Philo (a Jewish philosopher in Alexandria). The same basic thesis, although with different explanations for the idea of a Jesus figure, has been promoted by Albert Kalthoff, Arthur Drews, and others.

It may come as somewhat of a surprise that non-Christian historians of the first century make little mention of Christ or Christianity. In the dawn of the Christian era, pagan Rome paid little attention to what it considered to be simply another sect on the fringe of Judaism. Josephus, the Jewish historian who became attached to the court at Rome about A.D. 70, was reluctant to call attention to a minority group whose allegiance to "another king" could be misconstrued as Jewish opposition to the emperor.

There does exist, however, perfectly reliable historical evidence of the man Jesus Christ. In his *Antiquities* (xviii.3.3) Josephus speaks of Christ's miracles, His sentencing by Pilate, and His resurrection. A Talmudic tractate (*Sanhedrin* 43a) tells when and under what conditions Christ was put to death.

Pliny, the governor of Bithynia, in a letter to the emperor (about A.D. 110) reports that Christians made it a habit to meet before daybreak and ":recite a hymn antiphonally to Christ, as to a god." Both Tacitus, the most famous historian of Imperial Rome, and Suetonius, the private secretary of Hadrian, make direct reference to Christ (cf. Bettenson, *Documents of the Christian Church*, Oxford, 1963). (The best recent book on the subject of extrabiblical references to Jesus is F. F. Bruce, *Jesus and Christian Origins Outside the New Testament*, Eerdmans, 1974.) Thus we are by no means without objective extrabiblical evidence of the historicity of Jesus Christ.

I've heard it said recently that we can't know for sure what Jesus was like or what He said because all our information comes from New Testament writers who altered His sayings. Is this so?

While few critics deny the historicity of Jesus, many are in doubt as to how many of His sayings, as they now occur in the Gospels, are what He actually said. Criticism has led to considerable skepticism about the authenticity of almost all His teachings as recorded in the New Testament.

The question posed is rather complex and requires a fuller explanation than I can give here. May I suggest F. F. Bruce's widely read *The New Testament Documents: Are they Reliable?* (Eerdmans, 1959) and the more recent book, *The New Testament and Criticism,* (Eerdmans, 1967) by George Eldon Ladd. Moody Press has published a paperback called *Can I Trust My Bible?* which treats the subject in eight essays by conservative scholars.

The hypothesis that the early Christians began with a man Jesus and transformed Him into a supernatural Christ (the view underlying the question posed) has a number of weaknesses. The Christian faith arose in hostility, developed against opposition, and flowered in persecution.

Competent historians demand a cause sufficient for the effect. A well-intentioned teacher, later deified by misinformed followers, is hardly a plausible explanation.

A careful and sympathetic reading of the Gospels betrays no compulsive effort on the part of its authors to erect a theological superstructure on a mythical foundation. The accounts are, in fact, remarkably straightforward presentations of the life, death, and resurrection of Jesus Christ. Assuming the existence of God and His desire to redeem man, the New Testament strikes one as exactly what one might expect. If the authors "altered His sayings," the real question is why they didn't carry out their changes more noticeably.

Can you cite a couple of examples where archaeology has actually confirmed the accuracy of the Bible?

Since the essential truthfulness of Christianity does not lie in the realm of external verification, it is better to think of archaeology as illustrating or illuminating the Bible rather than confirming it. However, in areas where the biblical record has been held to have been in error and the spade of the archaeologist has vindicated its reliability, then it is proper to speak of archaeology as having "confirmed" the historical narrative.

Following are two examples, one which throws light on the text and the other which confirms its accuracy. First, in Ephesians 2:14 Paul speaks of the "dividing wall of hostility" which in former times had separated Jew and Gentile, but now in Christ was broken down. We now know that the source of Paul's metaphor was the low stone barrier which separated the court of the Gentiles from the inner court of the temple enclosure. This stone barrier was unearthed late in the nineteenth century by the French orientalist, Clermont-Ganneau. An inscription engraved in capital letters forbade foreigners from entering within the barrier and added, "Anyone who is caught doing so will be personally responsible for his ensuing death."

Second, for many years critics assumed that Luke was guilty of a historical faux pas when he located the enrollment which took Mary and Joseph to Bethlehem during the governorship of Quirinius (Luke 2:2). All secular information indicated that Saturninus was governor of Syria during that period and that Quirinius did not rule until some twelve years later. However, an inscription was discovered at Tiber which said that Quirinius *twice* governed as an imperial legate. Other data indicate that during the time when Jesus was born, both men were involved in governing Syria—Saturninus in a civil capacity and Quirinius as a military governor in connection with the Homonadensian War. At a later period Quirinius was civil governor, as mentioned in the secular material but not in any scriptural account.

If a knowledge of the "original Greek" clears up all questions, why are the experts still arguing?

I sympathize with those lay students of Scripture who are from time to time put down by someone who has studied a bit of Greek and settles every argument with the *shibboleth*, "The original Greek says . . ." As your question implies, a knowledge of the Greek text does not solve all the problems. For example, to know the Greek of I John 3:9 does little to explain why those born of God do not sin "for his *sperma* (seed? nature? the Holy Spirit?) remaineth in him."

A knowledge of Greek does, however, shed considerable light on texts which are fatally ambiguous in translation. It helps to separate the real problems from those which necessarily accompany even the best translation. One example occurs in the so-called Judgment of Nations passage (Matt. 25:31-46). Verse 32 says that all the nations shall be gathered before the Son of man and "he shall separate *them* one from another." Who will be separated? Apparently the nations. But the Greek text says *autous* (masculine) rather than *auta* (neuter) which would have corresponded with the gender of *ethna* (nations) which is neuter. This simple observation from the Greek text indicates that in the last days God will separate, not the nations, but the individuals who constitute the nations.

Why do equally well-trained scholars hold different positions on such issues as the rapture of the church, the millennium, and eternal security?

I sympathize with the frustration a layman must feel when he turns to several biblical scholars for the answer to a theological question and receives several different answers. Shouldn't the experts agree?

Reflect a moment, however, on "experts" in other fields. Economic theorists are unable to agree on the cure for inflation. Medical doctors may differ on their diagnosis of particular symptoms. Even automobile mechanics may be divided in their opinion about why your car misses when under load. To be an expert does not mean to know everything.

Let's look a bit closer at the biblical experts. One man may have as his major professional concern a thorough knowledge of the original language. He may have written his doctoral dissertation on the prepositions of the New Testament. Ask him almost anything about the intricacies of Hellenistic Greek and he will give you a thorough and dependable answer.

It does not follow, however, that he is especially knowledgeable in New Testament theology. He may never have given much thought to such larger issues as the kingdom of God or the messianic secret. Although he teaches in the biblical division of a theological seminary, his training and interests have not led him to a careful consideration of theological issues. But to the layman he is a New Testament expert.

Another consideration which accounts for difference in interpretation is the relationship of the question to the total theological orientation of the scholar. Most of us who have grown up in a somewhat ecclesiastical atmosphere come equipped with a theology given us by parents, Sunday school teachers, and pastors. This ready-made theology needs careful inspection, but this normally takes a lifetime. In the meantime the larger orientation provided by these given theological assumptions exerts a certain amount of pressure on our understanding of particular points.

For example, when a person who believes that God assures the final perseverance of the saints whom He has chosen for redemption (the historic Calvinist position) reads that God has reconciled believers by His death to present them holy and blameless *provided they continue in the faith* (Col. 1:22-23), he will probably feel a twinge of interpretive guilt and assure his injured conscience that he will have to look into that verse to find out what it actually says.

If a sufficient number of this sort of episodes occurs, the person may find himself gradually shifting from his inherited theological stance into one which is specifically his own. In the meantime, however, he will be answering questions in such a way as not to do violence to his larger theological position.

Questions about the rapture and the millennium pose two different problems. The first is called eisegesis (reading into Scripture). For some, the voice from heaven which says to John, "Come up hither, and I will show you what must take place after this" (Rev. 4:1), indicates the rapture of the church. It is quite clear to others that if you don't believe in the pretribulation rapture on other bases, you can't find it here.

In the case of the millennium it is a matter of sensitivity to literary genre. In a book where almost all the numbers seem to have symbolic value (7 seals, trumpets, bowls, etc. 144,000 Israelites; 42 months/1,260 days/3½ years) should not 1,000 years indicate a long period of time rather than a definite number of calendar years?

The interpreter will undoubtedly take a position on this based upon his larger approach to all Scripture. He will be inclined toward either a literalistic or a figurative interpretation. Both positions may be held in good faith. Ultimately, what we all wish to know is what the original writer had in mind when he penned Revelation 20:1-6.

Interpretation is both an art and a science. As a science we discuss such items as etymology, syntax, and grammar. As an art we go beyond the bare words and try to hear as clearly as possible what is really being said. So if interpreters differ, we would hope that they are doing their best to move from where they are to where in their best judgment the text is trying to take them.

What is the comparative value of various recent translations?

It is easy to understand why people want to

know whether one translation is better or more accurate than another. Words such as *idiomatic*, *paraphrase*, and *equivalency* are batted about and understood differently by different people. It may be helpful to set down some fundamental observations on New Testament translation.

1. There is no such thing as a "totally accurate" translation. Every school boy who has studied French or German, Greek or Latin, knows that there are no exact equivalents between words in one language and their counterparts in another. He knows that, at best, word meanings between languages are approximate and that words carry cultural connotations which, apart from a narrative exposition accompanying the text, cannot be transmitted with any degree of accuracy. How, for example, can the English word "peace" carry over the rich meaning of the Greek *eirēnē* with its debt to the Hebrew *shalom* which in turn so often has the overtones of Messianic salvation (Isa. 52:7; Acts 10:36)?

There is no such thing as a word-for-word translation. In the first place, individual words have numerous meanings. In English, for example, a door may be shut *fast*, you may have a *fast* friend, an airplane may be *fast*, cloth that doesn't fade is *fast*, etc. While there is a common element in each usage, the meanings are distinct. In Greek, for example, *katergadzomai* may mean to achieve, to create, to prepare, or to overpower. Thus, there is no single word in English which can be chosen ahead of time to be used in every case. Furthermore, as soon as you choose one of several alternatives you have departed from any idea of mechanical or "scientific" translation and entered the realm of interpretation.

2. The word order in Greek is inevitably different from any readable translation in English. A literal translation of Galatians 2:20a would be, "Christ I have been crucified with, I live yet, no longer I, lives but in me Christ." This distribution of words in Greek is not accidental. A good translator must find some way to carry over the Greek emphasis which places the word Christ first in the sentence. Perhaps, "It is with Christ that I have been crucified" would accomplish this. Knox has it, "With Christ I hang upon the cross." There is simply no way to avoid the fact that a good translation is at the same time a concise commentary.

3. A certain tension exists between the desire to make a translation modern and understandable and the necessity to keep in the reader's mind the fact that he is handling a piece of ancient literature which requires, for its proper understanding, an ancient setting. Phillips's oft-quoted "shake hands all around" for "greet one another with a holy kiss" (I Cor. 16:20) makes good sense in the contemporary suburban church, but eliminates

an important and meaningful liturgical expression of Christian love which prevailed in the first centuries of Christendom. It is questionable whether in the trade-off for modernity the recent translations haven't bartered away far too much of their rich heritage.

4. Christian theology must never rest on the shaky foundation of being one language removed from the original. To safeguard what God said through the prophets and apostles we must approach it in its original historical and grammatical setting. This does not mean that people should cease reading the Bible in English. It does mean, however, that for maximum accuracy revealed truth must be studied in the original languages.

Great benefit has come from modern language translations. Read them and enjoy them. But keep in mind the problems of translation and before committing yourself to some particular wording as truth, check it out in a good commentary based on the Greek text.

Are the alternate readings in the margins of the King James Version the work of the original translators?

They are the work either of the original translators or of subsequent editors. These alternate readings represent different possible meanings for the word or phrase being translated. Sometimes they represent variants in the original text itself. In the case of the New Testament, most people know that there are thousands of variant readings in the multitude of Greek manuscripts we have in hand. The purpose of textual criticism is to restore as accurately as possible a text which represents the nonexistent original. For those who are interested, Bruce Metzger has an excellent book on the subject, *The Text of the New Testament* (Oxford, 1964).

In the lengthy preface to the King James Version the translators resist the argument that alternate readings cast doubt on the authority of Scripture. Where the meaning of a word or phrase is uncertain, or where manuscript evidence is evenly divided between two readings, it is better to warn the reader than to leave the false impression of certainty. The King James translators criticized Pope Sixtus V for his decision that no variants should be listed in his edition of the Vulgate. (cf. F. F. Bruce, *The English Bible*, Oxford, 1970 pp. 101-106).

How can the translations of I Thessalonians 4:4 differ so much?

When translations are studied side by side one becomes aware of the relatively wide differences that may exist. Very little comparison is necessary to convince the student that translation is an art as well as a science.

In the King James Version the verse in question reads, "That every one of you should know how to possess his vessel in sanctification and honour." The crux of the problem is the meaning of the Greek *skeuos* in this context. Literally it means "vessel" but in our text it is used in a metaphorical sense. Weymouth is representative of the earlier modern speech translations and, following the King James Version, translates, "That each one of you shall know how to procure himself a wife." On the other hand, more recent translations tend to take *skeuos* to mean "body." Conybeare has "that each of you should learn to master his own body."

The variant translations of this verse supply a good example of the kind of problem that faces the translator in almost every verse. One approach is to translate in a straightforward way, taking each word in its primary dictionary sense. The result is normally a rather wooden and often ambiguous rendition. One reason why so many of the modern versions are more understandable than their predecessors is that they have decided not to pass on ambiguities of this sort. Where several interpretations are possible they accept the one which seems best and translate with clarity. While clarity is almost always desirable, the price in this case may be too high. How is the reader to know that other alternatives are possible? Someone has said (and I don't necessarily agree, although the point is well stated) that translations are like women—if beautiful they're not faithful; if faithful they're not beautiful.

If the older versions are correct in their understanding of *skeuos* then the passage is an admonition to live in a restrained and righteous manner with one's wife. If the word is to be taken as a metaphor for "body" then it is a charge to exercise control over one's bodily desires. The best procedure is to read what the better commentaries have to say about the verse and then adopt the translation which seems more probable to you.

In a recently published book, *The Battle for the Bible* by Harold Lindsell, I was surprised to come upon a section titled, "Alleged Errors by Robert H. Mounce." I have read your column for years and always thought you held a very high view of Scripture. Could you shed some light on the matter?

In the June 1966 issue of *Eternity*, shortly before I joined the staff as question-and-answer man, I wrote an article, "Clues to Understanding Biblical Accuracy." In the article I presented several examples of what others took to be errors in the Bible. In each case I demonstrated that they were not errors. Most so-called errors result from the modern mind trying to press upon the details of Scripture a standard of precision (whether mathematical or literary) alien to the cultural setting in which the Bible was written.

For example, we need not insist that since the "round" vessel of II Chronicles 4:2 has a diameter of "ten cubits," its circumference *must* be 565.48666+ inches, since $C = \pi$ d! The biblical "thirty cubits" (or 540 inches) is a reasonable and acceptable approximation (less than 5 percent difference).

In the book you mention, the author has misunderstood the major point I was making in that portion of the article—that is, that the four examples cited were alleged *by others* as "errors." But *I* insisted they *were not* errors. Unfortunately, the book contains such misleading statements as, "Mounce is looking hard to find an error," and, "In plain English, he is saying he has found a demonstrable error." (Copies of my original article are available at no cost: write *Eternity*, 1716 Spruce Street, Philadelphia, PA 19103.)

So in answer to your question, unless the word *error* is improperly skewed to represent some fine distinction inappropriately applied to Scripture, I continue to stand firmly, as I have written the author of the book in question, "on the side of an errorless Bible."

2
"Contradictions" in Scripture

One of the most overworked arguments against the Bible is that it is full of contradictions. The sheer repetition of this complaint would lead the uninformed to believe that Scripture is a hodgepodge of mutually exclusive statements.

Even a cursory knowledge of the Bible is enough to dispel that myth. The theological unity of its sixty-six books written over a period of some fifteen hundred years by more than forty authors is without precedent. The so-called discrepancies of Scripture are normally related to peripheral concerns and tend to fade away upon closer study.

In discussing the question, "Is the New Testament Historically Accurate?" (*Can I Trust My Bible?*, Moody Press, 1963), I wrote that "A. A. Hodge, a famous theologian who taught at Princeton, defined a discrepancy as a statement in the original text designed to set forth as true that which is absolutely contradictory to other statements in the original text or to definitely ascertained elements of human knowledge. In other words, *proving* the existence of a contradiction is not as easy as one might imagine. First of all, the 'erroneous statement' must be shown to be in the original text; then that the secular record was incontestably correct; and finally that the two are *essentially incapable* of being harmonized. To chat about 'contradictions' is one thing; to prove them is something else" (pp. 176-77).

This chapter deals with alleged contradictions in Scripture. More could be brought forward but these are typical. Hopefully the reader will come away with an understanding of why apparent discrepancies exist and how they yield to a fuller understanding when looked at more closely.

How do you explain science's vast difference in time (with reference to creation) from the biblical record?

The idea that the world was created in 4004 B.C. is not taught in the Bible. It is part of the chronological scheme worked out by the Archbishop of Armagh, Ireland, James Ussher (1581-1656). His computations were made on the basis of genealogies such as those found in Genesis 5 and 11.

Careful research since the time of Ussher indicates that genealogies of antiquity trace a general line of descent rather than supply a complete father-son list. Matthew 1:1 is an example of this telescoping process: "The book of the genealogy of Jesus Christ, the son of David, the son of Abraham."

The Bible is not in conflict with science's early dating of the appearance of man. It makes no scientific statement about the date of the primal pair. Rather, its truths are theological. It tells us that the first man rebelled against his Creator, forfeited the companionship of God, and led the entire human race into a state of tragic alienation. How long ago it happened we do not know, but that it did happen is taught by Scripture and confirmed by experience.

Are there contradictions in the Bible? If so, should a Sunday school teacher point them out to his students?

A problem encountered by almost everyone involved in sharing his faith with someone who questions the validity of the Christian faith is the problem of contradictions in Scripture. I can remember the impact of a professor pointing out to our college class the "mathematical error" in I Kings 7:23 in which the brazen sea (a circular basin or tank) was "ten cubits from brim to brim, round in compass . . . and a line of thirty cubits compassed it round about." Since the circumference of a circle is the diameter times pi (c= π d), a ten cubit diameter would have to yield a circumference of more than thirty cubits (10 times 3.14159265, etc. equals at least 31)! Not every apparent difficulty in Scripture is that simple to understand— obviously the ten and thirty are round numbers.

It is true that there are apparent contradictions in the Bible. This fact has caused considerable concern among those who accept the Bible as the Word of God and want to commit themselves wholeheartedly to its teachings.

The responses to this problem have been several. Some have given up in despair and decided that what they can't understand they will leave alone. The usual illustration is that of the man-eating fish who enjoys the meat but pushes the bones aside. Isaiah 55:9 ("So are my ways higher than your ways and my thoughts than your thoughts") is quoted in support of this attitude.

At the other end of the spectrum are what A. W. Tozer calls "rationalistic-orthodox theologians" who "in fancied near-omniscience presume to resolve all biblical difficulties with a wave of their typewriter" (*The Root of the Righteous* pp. 77-78). The problem with this approach is its implicit assumption that Scripture must at every point yield to our standards of consistency and that failure at any point, no matter how unimportant in itself, will destroy the logical basis for trust in the Bible.

Somewhere between these extremes is a more commonsense approach that neither assigns all problems to the realm of mystery or frenetically pursues absolute harmonization. The Bible is an ancient book and resists being interpreted in a culture not its own. Research has thrown light on many ancient customs which in turn have provided insight into biblical incongruities which have long vexed the expositor. Some "contradictions" result from our own insistence upon making Scripture conform to twentieth-century standards.

To what extent these problems should be pointed out to students depends, of course, on their age and intellectual maturity. It is my opinion that too often we evade (or whitewash) the problems and inadvertently leave them to be wrestled with under less favorable circumstances.

How do you reconcile the fact that although our sins are removed "as far as the east is from the west" (Ps. 103:12), on the day of judgment we will give account of every careless word we utter (Matt. 12:36)?

That God forgives all who turn to Him in faith is a cardinal doctrine of Scripture. This forgiveness is grounded upon the shed blood of Christ (Eph. 1:7) and is the supreme expression of the mercy of God. Apart from the unpardonable sin (Matt. 12:31) there is no sin that God cannot forgive.

Even upon the cross Christ said of those who had nailed him there, "Father, forgive them; for they know not what they do" (Luke 23:34). To Israel God said, "I have swept away your transgressions like a cloud, and your sins like mist" (Isa. 44:22) and through Jeremiah He promised, "I will forgive their iniquity, and I will remember their sin no more" (Jer. 31:34).

Against this background of total forgiveness it seems strange to hear reminders of future accountability. In addition to the saying of Jesus quoted in your question we should hear as well the stern admonition of Paul, "So each of us shall give account of himself to God" (Rom 14:12). Again in II Corinthians 5:10 Paul indicates the inevitability of future judgment for the believer when he writes "For we must all appear before the judgment seat of Christ, so that each one may receive good or evil, according to what he has done in the body."

The answer to this apparent contradiction lies along the following lines: On the one hand, God's forgiveness is full and complete. God grants pardons, he doesn't merely parole. The moment I turn from my sinful pride and independence which keeps me from his redeeming love, I experience a perfect and complete forgiveness. There are no ifs or maybes. Nothing remains unforgiven. Nor will God drag it out for some future reckoning.

On the other hand, Christian discipleship involves responsibility. The quality of our lives as measured in the most practical of terms will be assessed on the day of judgment. Paul distinctly says in Romans 2:6-7, "For he will render to every man according to his works: to those who by patience in well-doing seek for glory and honor and immortality, he will give eternal life." God has never promised the believer some sort of ethical carte blanche which allows him to do what he wants and be covered by a policy of automatic forgiveness. We are responsible, and responsibility involves a day of reckoning.

In I John 1:9 present tense *homologomen* suggests a translation such as, "As we continue to ask forgiveness for the sins we daily commit, he will faithfully respond in forgiveness and cleanse us from unrighteousness." Perhaps the crucial question is, Will *these* sins ever be brought up against us again? Or are only sins prior to salvation blotted out?

At the risk of climbing too far out on a theological limb, I would answer that any sin once forgiven has no further guilt attached to it. God forgives on the basis of the death of Christ and this great redemptive act has absorbed *all* punishment for sin. This does not mean, however, that the sinful act itself is somehow removed from history. The event remains and bears witness to our lack of Christian maturity or our unwillingness to obey at that specific point of our spiritual pilgrimage. In this sense, the "careless word" will play a part in the final reckoning. Even though forgiven it will always exist as an indicator of our life at that point. God does not rewrite history to make believers look better than they are. Forgiveness keeps the believer in fellowship with God but it does not obliterate the basis for evaluating the quality of his life.

I have noticed that sometimes a saying of Jesus is recorded differently when it is reported in more than one Gospel. How can this be if the Bible is inspired?

I remember what a surprise it was when I first discovered this very fact. I was studying a parallel edition of the Gospels and almost from the outset was faced with the problem that while the Gospel writers did not really change the gist of what Jesus said, they did not put the same words in His mouth. Somehow I felt that where Scripture introduced a saying with the formula "Jesus said" we should expect to have the very words of Jesus.

I am not sure whether I would have been

even more confused if I had known at the time that Jesus did not speak in the language in which the New Testament was written. At the very first stage of transmission, translation into a foreign language was involved.

It will be well to supply an example or two for purposes of comparison. Matthew 9:2: "Take heart, my son; your sins are forgiven." Mark 2:5: "My son, your sins are forgiven." Luke 5:20: "Man, your sins are forgiven you."

Matthew 24:15: "So when you see the desolating sacrilege spoken of by the prophet Daniel, standing in the holy place." Mark 13:14: "But when you see the desolating sacrilege set up where it ought not to be." Luke 21:20: "But when you see Jerusalem surrounded by armies, then know that its desolation has come near."

It is obvious that these parallel passages are not verbally the same. It is also obvious that they nevertheless communicate the same basic idea. The question raised is how can we accept the verbal differences yet maintain a doctrine of inspiration. It would seem that Jesus either said exactly what the Gospel writer wrote that He said or He did not. In that case, if Mark is accurate, how could Matthew or Luke give us a different set of words?

The doctrine of inspiration has to do with the superintending activity of the Holy Spirit upon men chosen by God so that what they wrote is trustworthy and authoritative (cf. Carl Henry's article on inspiration in *Baker's Dictionary of Theology*, Baker, 1960, pp. 286-89). Inspiration does not guarantee that the Gospel writers recorded the *ipsissima verba* (the very words) of Jesus. It is theoretically possible that a saying of Jesus could be accurately communicated by any one of several arrangements of words and phrases. Each would say the same, but none would be exactly like another. Inspiration guarantees only that the way each writer chose to record the saying did not distort the meaning or in any way diminish the authority of the utterance. Inspiration provides us with an accurate and reliable account of what was said or done. The choice of individual words and their arrangement into meaningful phrases is the work of the writer.

One additional consideration should be noted. Since we have none of the original documents of the New Testament, how can we be sure that copyists down through the centuries have not distorted our Scripture? Once again, it is not the doctrine of inspiration that safeguards the transmission of the text. It can be argued, of course, that if God inspired the original writing of Scripture He would also see to it that it would be accurately preserved in transmission. We do have, however, thanks to the continuing labors of textual critics, a remarkably accurate restoration of the original text. Some five thousand

Greek manuscripts, in part or in whole, are available for the painstaking work of reconstructing a text which for all practical purposes is a copy of the original. While inspiration does not authenticate the reconstructed text, the science of textual criticism has placed in our hands what must be considered a working duplicate of the original. An accurate copy of the inspired original gives us confidence that the sayings of Jesus as recorded by the synoptists provide us with the *ipsissima vox* (voice) *Jesu* if not His *ipsissima verba*.

Will you please explain John 1:18, "No one has ever seen God," in light of Exodus 33:11 which claims that "The Lord used to speak to Moses face to face"?

One of the remarkable things about the Word of God is that it makes no attempt to evade apparent contradictions. Its simplicity and straightforwardness is an eloquent testimony to the honesty and reliability of its writers. That "contradictions" have a way of resolving themselves upon closer study is a strong argument for the inspiration of Scripture. The case in point is an excellent example.

The ancient world would readily agree with John that God in His essential being is inaccessible to sense perception—He cannot be seen. Many years before Plato had said, "Never man and God can meet." The Church in Asia Minor would accept without question the assertion that no man had ever seen God.

How then shall we interpret Exodus 33:11 which seems to say the opposite? Again we need to look at context. Whenever Moses went outside the camp and entered into the tabernacle, a pillar of cloud came down and stood at the door. The voice was that of God who spoke "face to face, *as a man speaks to his friend*." Here the second phrase explains the first. "Face to face" means "not from the distant heaven, but closely and directly as in familiar conversation." The question is not whether Moses looked at God's face but whether God spoke from some lofty height or intimately as a man speaks to his friend. The verse does not demand physical sight. In fact, a few verses later God tells Moses, "You cannot see my face; for man shall not see me and live" (v. 20). As the human eye is blinded by gazing directly into the sun so would mortal man perish before a direct and unveiled disclosure of the glory of God.

Why do Matthew and Luke differ in the order of Jesus' temptations?

To study the first three Gospels side by side is an interesting and illuminating experience. One of the first things one discovers is that the writers are not nearly as concerned with historical sequence as we might be. For the Gospel writers, the significance of events took priority over their historical sequence.

Comparing the temptation accounts in Matthew and Luke we find that the second and third are reversed in order (Luke places universal sovereignty before angelic protection). Although Matthew is more prone to topical arrangement, he is the one who supplies the specific words which suggest sequence ("then," Matt. 4:5, "again," Matt. 4:8).

It may be best to follow the clue in Mark's passing reference, ("He was in the wilderness forty days, tempted by Satan," Mark 1:13) which definitely implies that the temptations continued throughout the entire forty days. (The periphrastic construction with the present participle in the Greek supports this interpretation.)

If this be the case the matter of sequence relates to the stylized telling of the story and not to the temptations themselves conceived of as three specific events in point of time.

Why did Jesus at the wedding of Cana rebuke His mother saying, "My hour has not yet come" (John 2:4), yet perform the miracle anyway?

The response of Jesus on this occasion is enigmatic to say the least. A literal translation of the Greek text would be, "What to me and to thee, woman?" (*Ti emoi kai soi, gunai*).

This may be understood as meaning: 1) "This is no concern of ours"; or 2) in the words of the New English Bible, "Your concern, mother, is not mine." The majority of expositors favor the latter interpretation and see in Jesus' answer a mild rebuke. Mary is understood as encouraging Jesus to do something which would call attention to Himself and further His messianic mission.

I personally favor the first interpretation, not only because it is the more natural reading of the Greek text, but because the entire incident is more adequately understood as another phase of the wilderness temptation. Once again Jesus faces the subtle suggestion to perform a miracle for personal advantage. Mary turns to Jesus, not to egg Him on to a display of His miracle-working ability, but because the host was embarrassed by running out of wine and Jesus always knew what to do in situations like this. The adversary is Satan, not a scheming woman.

Incidentally, the expression "woman" is not a rebuke. The Greek *gunai* occurs, for instance, in John 19:26 where Jesus from the cross says, "Woman (*gunai*) behold your son."

The hour which had not yet come was the hour "for the Son of man to be glorified" (John 12:23; cf. John 13:1 and 17:1 where Jesus prays, "Father, the hour has come; glorify thy Son that the Son may glorify thee").

The messianic mission of Jesus was not to be achieved by a spectacular display of miraculous power, but by obedience to the

Father's will which led through the valley of humiliation and death on its way to final exaltation.

Parables like that of the mustard seed (Matt. 13:31, 32) are very optimistic about the growth of Christianity, yet other verses, such as Matthew 7:13, 14 ("The way is hard that leads to life, and those who find it are few"), seem to teach the opposite. How can these opposing perspectives be harmonized, and how does all this relate to the modern emphasis on renewal in the church?

I don't think it is necessary—and perhaps not even wise—to harmonize what seem to be differing perspectives within Scripture. Could it not be that our anxiety for immediate consistency often robs us of the impact of a particular biblical teaching? Let the obvious point sink in and do its work rather than be weakened by secondary considerations. The Bible is an Eastern book and we are Westerners. Our prosaic turn of mind is often uneasy as Scripture roams unhindered in the realm of metaphor and paradox. Our syllogistic mentality is embarrassed when the the Word of God persuades existentially rather than logically. I rather think that part of accepting the Bible as the Word of God is to stop asking it to prove itself at every single point.

Now back to your example. It is true, is it not, that the kingdom of God has grown from a mustard seed beginning (a few disciples and some women) to a great universal tree? Does not history tell the story of a most remarkable expansion of what was quite obscure in its origins? The church exists in innumerable cultures and includes those of every race. It began in a particular setting; it is now universal in scope.

At the same time, the gate is narrow, the way is hard, and few there are who find it. The gate is narrow in that it can be entered only by those who are genuinely repentant of their sins. It is hard in the sense that, infected by sin, we would continually wander from the way. Those who find life in Christ Jesus are few in comparison with the many who have chosen the easy way of self-interest which leads to destruction.

In regard to the other part of your question, the fact that only a few follow the hard way that leads to life has no real bearing on church renewal. Nor should it in any way affect the church's role in evangelism. It is the church's responsibility to proclaim the gospel, no matter how many or how few respond; it is God's responsibility to draw men to Himself.

How do you explain Jesus' severe denunciation of the Pharisees in Matthew 23 in view of His own command not to judge in Matthew 7:1?

The judging which Jesus speaks against is "the *habit* of censorious and carping criticism" (R.V.G. Tasker).

The Greek verb *krinō* occurs 114 times in the New Testament with considerable variation in meaning. Context must always be the final arbiter as to its exact nuance in a specific passage. In Matthew 7:1 two things are quite clear: 1) the admonition is directed against that kind of caustic and debilitating criticism which depresses and condemns; 2) the form of the prohibition (*mē* and the present infinitive) indicates a continuing habit which must be brought to a halt.

In Matthew 23 Jesus directs His rebuke against that kind of Pharisaic distortion which kept men out of the kingdom (v. 13), elevated ritual trivia over the great principles of genuine religion (v. 23), and camouflaged inner moral decay with a whitewashed exterior (v. 27).

As a reformer Jesus burned with righteous indignation over the ecclesiastical betrayal of the great religious and ethical heritage of the people of God. It was time for an objective appraisal of all aspects of Pharisaism, both good and bad. To see Jesus in this role is to feel the full impact of His criticism without committing oneself to the ridiculous proposition that every Pharisee was a destestable hypocrite.

When Jesus was on the cross, He was offered some vinegar, presumably drugged. Matthew 27:48 and Mark 15:36 say, "gave it to him to drink"; Matthew 27:34 says, "when he tasted it, he would not drink it"; John 19:29-30 says, "when Jesus had received the vinegar." Did He, or did He not, drink it?

The verses listed involve two incidents. Matthew 27:34 refers to the custom of giving to the victim to be crucified a narcotic wine (*oinon meta choles memigmenon*) to dull his senses. This took place about nine o'clock in the morning. Jesus did not drink this wine, choosing rather to be in full possession of His faculties.

It was some six hours later after the agonizing struggle with sin that he cried, "I thirst" (John 19:28) and was given a mild vinegar-wine (*oksous*, v. 30; *oksos*, according to Abbott-Smith, p. 319, is "the ordinary drink of laborers and common soldiers"). This he took perhaps to moisten parched lips and provide a momentary stimulant for the great and final redemptive proclamation, "It is finished."

The statements in Matthew 27:48 and

Mark 15:36 are parallel and belong to the second incident. They speak of the cruelty of the soldiers in temporarily withholding the wine from Christ to see if Elijah would come and save Him. It is John who indicates that Jesus eventually received the wine.

Are I Corinthians 7:1 and I Corinthians 16:20 contradictory?

The two verses in question are "It is good for a man not to touch a woman" and "Greet one another with a holy kiss." At first glance they certainly seem to qualify as contradictory. It is pretty hard to kiss without touching! Both verses, however, need to be understood against the cultural background. The "holy kiss" was a perfectly normal greeting in biblical times. In fact, it is still practiced extensively throughout many European countries. In the Western world we shake hands instead of bussing one another on the cheek. It is a matter of cultural difference. J. B. Phillips has translated the verse in modern idiom: "I should like you to shake hands all around as a sign of Christian love."

The element of apparent contradiction is removed when we understand I Corinthians 7:1 correctly. To "touch a woman" does not mean a casual or accidental contact but is a euphemism for sexual relations. Beck translates, "It is good for a man not to have sex relations with a woman." There was a rather widespread admiration for celibacy in Paul's day and the apostle is agreeing that in view of the impending distress (v. 26) it is a desirable state (cf. v. 7).

How can you reconcile Paul's teaching on love in I Corinthians 13:5 ("Love does not insist on its own way") with the "sharp contention" which he had with Barnabas over the advisability of taking John Mark along on the second missionary journey (Acts 15:39)?

In the first place, it is important to understand that God does not necessarily approve of all the actions recorded in the Bible. This is true not only of the actions of unbelievers, but also of the early church and even the apostles.

For instance, the Christians at Corinth were wrong in their division into factions (I Cor. 1:10–13), their lack of concern regarding immorality within the church (ch. 5), and their abuse of the Lord's Supper (11:20-22). Peter was most certainly wrong when, at Antioch upon the arrival of certain Jews from Jerusalem, he separated himself from table fellowship with the Gentiles (Gal. 2:11-21).

In the same way it would seem that both Paul and Barnabas were at fault in allowing their difference of opinion about John Mark to climax in a "sharp contention." (The Greek *paroksusmos* is a strong term, as is the following verb, *apōchoristhēnai*, "to depart asunder.")

To say that since the contention resulted in two missionary teams instead of one it must therefore have been right, is to confuse Christian ethics with God's graciousness in overruling human blunders. The end has never justified the means.

That both Paul and Barnabas held opposing views is both understandable and acceptable. John Mark, who had begun the journey in good faith but turned back upon reaching what seemed to him to be the geographical borders of heathendom, was not in Paul's estimation the man to take along on the second trip. Evidently Barnabas felt that a change had taken place in Mark and that he should be given another chance.

However, whatever the reasons may have been on either side of the question, it is safe to say that the entire matter should have been resolved without such an abrupt parting. It is good to note that whatever feelings existed at the moment did not continue indefinitely. In Colossians 4:10 Paul sends the greetings of "Mark the cousin of Barnabas" and in II Timothy 4:11 he asks that Mark be brought to him "for he is very useful in serving me."

3
Difficult Passages: Genesis —Acts

People often forget that the Bible is an ancient book. It was written against a cultural background quite distinct from our own. The Israelites lived in a world in which human sacrifice, polygamy, and the absolute sovereignty of kings were accepted cultural practices. Even in New Testament times the "exposure" of female infants was a secular custom which met no legal opposition.

Little wonder, then, that the Bible contains a number of difficult passages. With the passing of time even the Jewish people misunderstood Moses' regulation, "You shall not boil a kid in its mother's milk" (Exod. 23:19), making it the basis for kosher laws when in fact we now know, thanks to the discoveries at Ugarit in 1939, that it was probably only a prohibition against involvement in a certain Canaanitish religious practice.

The next two chapters deal with difficult verses. Many more could be added to the list, but these are the ones that over the past few years have been brought to my attention. In addition to suggesting plausible interpretations for specific problem passages, I am hopeful that the following discussions will develop a methodology for answering other troublesome verses in Scripture.

Why did God curse Canaan (Gen. 9:25) when it was his father Ham who sinned against Noah?

This question comes from the account which tells of Ham's improper reaction upon finding his father drunk in his tent. When the other two brothers, Shem and Japheth, learned from Ham of their father's nakedness they entered the tent backwards and covered him. Noah awoke from his wine and "knew what his youngest son had done to him," so he cursed Canaan (his grandson) instead of Ham (the apparent culprit).

The usual answer to this injustice is that the sins of the father are visited on the children. The effects of sin extend not only to one's own progeny but to society as a whole. Thus, the curse on Canaan was a prediction of that which history would soon bear out.

An alternate, and more probable, interpretation is that Canaan also learned of

Noah's nakedness and performed some shameful act which is not recorded. The expression "his youngest son" more literally means "the little (one)" and could refer to Canaan as well as Ham. Thus Canaan is being punished for his own sin and not that of his father.

Does the commandment, "You shall not kill" (Exod. 20:13) mean that Christians are not to go to war?

That the sixth commandment is to be understood as a prohibition against murder and is not a blanket condemnation of the taking of life under any circumstance is seen by the fact that God not only authorized capital punishment ("Whoever sheds the blood of man, by man shall his blood be shed; for God made man in his own image"; Gen. 9:6), but also sent his people into war ("Now go and smite Amalek, and utterly destroy all that they have"; I Sam. 15:3). This does not mean that God views physical life as cheap. It means rather that as important as life is, it is not the highest of all values. If a choice must be made between the life of one and justice to many, Scripture seems to take the second alternative.

The principle that physical life must be subordinated to higher values is easy to see on a personal level. Who wouldn't defend his wife or mother from criminal assault? What

is more difficult to see is that the same principle is equally valid in a more complex social
situation. If Paul is right in his assertion that
properly instituted authority is the "servant
of God to execute his wrath on the wrong-
doer" (Rom. 13:4), then international aggression and exploitation are to be resisted on the
authority of God (cf. Rom. 13:1-2).

To determine when men ought to take up
arms against another nation has always been
a terribly complicated decision, but that
armed resistance is a permissible ingredient
in the unhappy history of man is acknowledged
by Scripture.

In I Samuel 16:14-15 we read about an "evil spirit from God." How can anything but good come from a God of love?

Most commentators answer this problem by
pointing out that the ancient Hebrews interpreted all of life as under the direct control
of God. Amos 3:6 is often quoted: "Does evil
befall a city, unless the Lord has done it?"

The mood of pathological melancholy
which settled over Saul was understood as a
divine visitation, even though the result was
evil. It was God who had removed his Spirit
(v. 14) and it was equally God who sent retribution upon Saul for his rejection of the
divine command (cf. 15:23, 26).

Some textual scholars have conjectured
that this is a classic example of scribal

emendation. Originally the text would have said, "the spirit from the Lord tormented him." A scribe, uneasy about attributing this questionable activity to God, suggested in the margin an alternate, "an evil spirit from the Lord." The contextual difficulty with this conjecture is that verse 14 would originally have said that the Spirit of the Lord both "departed" and "tormented" Saul.

A straightforward reading of the text indicates two spirits, not one.

How could David say to God, "Against thee, thee only, have I sinned" (Ps. 51:4), when quite obviously he had also sinned against Bathsheba, Uriah her husband, Michal his own wife, and the whole nation of Israel?

Certainly David's prayer is not to be interpreted as an attempt to evade the social responsibility of his sin. He is not saying to God, "Well, I sinned against you, that's for sure, but I didn't hurt anyone else." David is fully aware of the social consequences of his act. Desire led to adultery, adultery to murder, murder to retribution in terms of the disintegration of the royal family.

What David is confessing is that, in an ultimate sense, sin not only works to the disadvantage of others but directs itself against God Himself. David is not denying the social consequences of his act but acknowledging that sin in essence is a betrayal of the divine trust. Sin is not the breaking of impersonal laws but the shattering of a personal relationship.

"Thee only" is a way of saying that no matter how detestable his actions toward Bathsheba and Uriah, the worst part of his sin was breaking trust with God. To be humanly concerned about the way our sin affects others is commendable. To realize that sin also wounds the heart of a loving God deepens our sense of sin immeasurably.

Who is Lucifer? In Isaiah 14:12 the Revised Standard Version calls him the day star. Is this Satan?

It is rather commonly thought that Lucifer is another name for Satan. A note in the Scofield Bible (p. 726) begins somewhat tentatively by saying that Isaiah 14:12-14 "evidently refers to Satan." This caution soon gives way to the more positive statement that Lucifer "can be none other than Satan" and that "this tremendous passage marks the beginning of sin in the universe."

The Hebrew word in question is *helel* which comes from a verb meaning "to shine." As a noun it occurs only once in the Old Testament and means "shining one" or, more specifically, "bright star." In Greek this "morning star" or "day star" was designated *heosphoros* (light bearer) and in Latin *lucifer* (from *lux*, light; and *ferre*, to bear.) The latter was the Latin name for the planet Venus which is most often our "morning star."

The popular identification with Satan came as a result of interpreting the Isaiah passage in light of Luke 10:18 ("I saw Satan fall like lightning from heaven"). The "falling" of Satan in Luke, however, refers to the triumph of the kingdom of God *during* the mission of the seventy, not to some original fall viewed by the preincarnate Christ.

The basic reason for rejecting the popular identification with Satan is that Isaiah 14:4 expressly directs the "tauntsong" which follows (cf. Hab. 2:6 for a similar use of the Hebrew *mashal*) against the king of Babylon. Whatever similarities the original fall of Satan may have had with the downfall of a proud and ambitious earthly monarch, the literal and primary interpretation of Isaiah 14 has to do with the king of Babylon. John Calvin put it rather bluntly when he said that to refer this passage to Satan is an instance of "very gross ignorance" and counselled his readers to pass by such improbable inventions as "useless fables."

In Matthew's genealogy of Christ (1:2-16) why does he mention four women: three of questionable moral standing (Tamar, Rahab, and Bathsheba "the wife of Uriah") and the fourth a foreigner (Ruth)?

Matthew obviously has more in mind in developing his genealogy than merely supplying the names which constituted the royal line. This follows from his arrangement of the names in three groups of fourteen each (cf. Matt. 1:17, but note that the third group has but thirteen generations) and the omission of Ahaziah, Joash, and Amaziah after Joram (v. 8) and Jehoiakim after Josiah (v. 11).

Perhaps the most satisfactory answer is that by the inclusion of the four women in the line of Christ the reader is prepared for the most outstanding fact of the entire genealogy— the virgin birth of Jesus. That is to say, by going out of his way to include the unusual, Matthew is setting the stage for the unique.

What does it mean to "hallow the name of God" (Matt. 6:9)?

I would imagine that most people who recite the first petition of the Lord's Prayer ("hallowed be thy name") would be hard put to give a full theological explanation of this request. Like so many of the concise utterances of Scripture, it does not yield itself readily apart from some background and definition. It is important that theological truth be understood rather than vaguely felt.

When we choose names for our children we usually decide on the basis of how they sound when placed with the last name, whether or not Uncle George would be pleased if we used his name, etc.

Not so in biblical times. A name was not simply a label: it was an expression of character. Names were changed when men were changed. At the brook Jabbok, Jacob ("he who clutches the heel," that is, the supplanter, Gen. 25:26) wrestled a man until the break of day and was renamed Israel ("for you have striven with God and with men, and have prevailed," Gen. 32:28). Simon was given the name Cephas (Aramaic for "rock," often occurring in the New Testament in the Greek form *petros*—Peter; cf. John 1:42). When the psalmist declared that while some trust in chariots and horses, God's people are to "boast of the name of the Lord our God" (Ps. 20:7). He is exhorting them to trust in the nature and character of God.

The petition, then, is that the character of God be "hallowed." The Greek word for hallowed means to set apart or to make holy. When used of God it means to reverence or to hold in highest esteem. Barclay puts the two ideas together and paraphrases, "Enable us to give to Thee the unique place Thy nature and character deserve and demand" (*The Gospel of Matthew*).

If we pay careful attention to the context, we may be able to bring the petition into sharper focus. Jesus has just instructed His disciples to address their prayer to "Our Father." The Aramaic *abba* (father) is taken from a child's vocabulary. According to the *Theological Dictionary of the New Testament* (Eerdmans, 1964-), the word *abba* was "an infant sound applied without inhibition to God." Thus the specific aspect of God's character which we are to hallow is His willingness to enter into a Father-son relationship with those who by faith belong to the family of God. The petition would then be, "Let thy character as *abba*, Father, be held in highest esteem."

It is possible (and even probable) that the final clause of Matthew 6:10 ("as in heaven, also upon earth") should be appended to each of the three preceding petitions. Thus the prayer would be that God's name be hallowed *on earth* as it is now being reverenced in heaven. (Compare the great throne room scene in Revelation 4 and the adoration of the heavenly multitude in Revelation 7.)

If this were so, how different life would be. So many of the difficulties which rob the believer of the sheer joy of living would vanish if God's character were being held in highest esteem right here on earth amidst the turmoil and perplexities of everyday life.

One example: Worry seems to dominate much of life. We worry about children, about finances, about job security, about our reputation, ad infinitum. Yet full awareness of the character of God as *abba*, Father, must of necessity dispel all such ignoble concern. To worry is to declare that God is either unable or unwilling to enter compassionately into our problem. He is neither. To hold His character in highest esteem right here on earth is to demonstrate by the quality of our lives that He is both able and willing to live up to His name. "Hallowed be thy name" is not a solemn dirge for ritual occasions but a practical exhortation for dynamic Christian living.

Explain Matthew 7:6: "Do not give dogs what is holy; and do not throw your pearls before swine."

In the Eastern world the dog was a scavenger. He ate whatever he could find wherever he found it. Thus for the Jewish community the dog became a symbol of complete disregard for dietary restrictions. Remember that Jesus said to the Syrophoenician woman (a Gentile), "It is not right to take the children's bread and throw it to the dogs" (Mark 7:27).

The pig, of course, was *terefah* (unacceptable by ritualistic standards) and could not be eaten. Hence, Jesus is here cautioning against indiscriminate sharing of the Christian faith. Pearls of great price (the more intimate truths of Christian faith and experience) are not to be exposed to those whose predictable response will be one of scorn and increased hostility. Pigs trample them underfoot and dogs turn to attack.

Explain Matthew 10:32-33: "So everyone who acknowledges me before men, I also will acknowledge before my father who is in heaven; but whoever denies me before men, I also will deny before my father who is in heaven."

In the immediate context this verse refers both to those who heard the Twelve in the course of their missionary journeys and to the Twelve themselves. The disciples were sent out with the message, "The kingdom of heaven is at hand" (v. 7). They were to go as sheep in the midst of wolves (v. 16). Persecution waited on every hand (vv. 17-28). But God who cares for the sparrows who fall and has numbered the hairs of man's head (vv. 29, 30) would protect them from the evil one.

Thus, acknowledge me before men; do not deny me, Jesus was saying. Those who carry through (cf. v. 22) will be acknowledged before God but those who in the face of persecution disown Christ will also be disowned by God. The same holds true for those who receive the message. Open acknowledgment leads to divine acceptance but denial to eternal disfavor.

How can Jesus say in Matthew 11:14 that John the Baptist is Elijah?

In Malachi 4:5 is the promise, "Behold, I will send you Elijah the prophet before the great and terrible day of the Lord comes." In Matthew 11:11ff. Jesus said that there is no man greater than John the Baptist and that if the people were willing to accept it, "[John] is Elijah who is to come." The essential problem that this equation poses is the nature of prophetic language. In common parlance the statement, "Mr. Brown is coming," means that Mr. Brown—not someone who looks or acts like him—is coming. But Jesus provides us with a concrete illustration that the language of prophecy may be taken in a much more figurative sense. Quite obviously He is *not* saying that John the Baptist is a reincarnation of the ancient prophet of Israel. Prophetic utterance is not a Dixonesque prediction of specific items yet to come. The point is that John the Baptist appears on the scene *in the power and spirit* of his prototype, Elijah. And in so doing, Elijah returns.

Mark 4:12 seems to say that Jesus spoke in parables so that people would not understand. How could this be?

Beginning in the middle of the preceding verse the passage reads, "For those outside everything is in parables; so that they may indeed see but not perceive, and may indeed hear but not understand; lest they should turn again, and be forgiven."

A quick check in any standard commentary will show that this statement has caused New Testament scholars considerable trouble. It seems strange that Jesus, the master teacher, should use a method of communication designed to *hide* the truth rather than to make it plain. The major problem is the expression "so that." It is possible linguistically to soften the Greek *hina* to mean "consequently." In this case the verse would simply indicate what happens when spiritual truths fall upon the ears of unbelievers. It is also possible to retranslate the underlying Aramaic *de* as a relative pronoun. This would turn "so that" into "who" and verse twelve would be no more than a description of the outsiders who turn away in unbelief.

The traditional view is that Jesus used the parable to *reveal* truth to those who wanted to learn while at the same time to *conceal* it from unbelievers for whom additional light would result in increased responsibility. A recent commentator, C. E. B. Cranfield, writes that

God's self-revelation must be a veiled revelation "in order that men may be left sufficient room in which to make a personal decision" (*Cambridge Greek Testament Commentary*, "Mark," Cambridge, p. 158). It is certainly God's will that men turn to Him for forgiveness, but not at the expense of violating their own will. Here, as elsewhere, God stands at the door and knocks.

Mark 10 says that if a person gets divorced and remarries, he or she will be committing adultery (vv. 11-12). Isn't that pretty severe?

Yes. In the previous paragraph Jesus taught that in marriage God creates a new entity ("the two shall become one," v. 8) and what God has so joined together, man is not to separate (v. 9). Moses had allowed a man to divorce his wife if he would write her a certificate of divorce, but the primary function of this decree was to provide some protection for the woman, not to allow the man to change wives at will. This provision was designed not to sanction divorce, but because of the hardness of their hearts (v. 5). It deals with a contingency brought about by human sinfulness.

Jesus' words emphasize the seriousness of the matter. To divorce and remarry is to commit adultery. Some have suggested that the qualifying clause in Matthew 19:9 ("except for unchastity"; cf. Matt. 5:32), should be understood in Mark as well. This would indicate that Jesus did not intend His command as severely as it appears in the Marcan account. In any case, Jesus clearly sets Himself against the whole idea of divorce in that it reverses the divine intention of lifelong commitment of a man and a woman.

What language was Jesus speaking in Mark 15:34 when He said, "Eloi, Eloi, lama sabachthani"? and what does the verse mean?

Jesus uttered these words from the cross in his native Galilean Aramaic. Aramaic was the language of the Arameans and long before the time of Christ it had become an international language from Italy to India. It achieved such widespread usage in part because of its syntactical flexibility, its simple script, and its capacity for absorbing foreign elements. Jesus' utterance occurs in a slightly different form in Matthew's account ("Eli, Eli"). This results from a separate attempt to transliterate (to spell out using the letters of another alphabet) the saying for a Greek audience. Bystanders misunderstood and thought Jesus was calling for Elijah—an understandable error.

Numerous explanations for this enigmatic saying have been proposed ("My God, my God, why hast thou forsaken me?"). One is that Jesus is merely reciting the opening verse of Psalm 22 as an act of devotion. Another is the conjecture that it reflects the intensity of His disappointment that God did not at this time of His greatest need reverse His fortune and usher in the new age. The traditional explanation is that the cry is to be taken theologically as revealing the awful separation of the Son from the Father when He took upon Himself the penalty and punishment for the sins of mankind (II Cor. 5:21).

Writing before the turn of the century, Ezra Gould noted that the historical meaning of *sabachthani* was not to leave *alone* but to leave *helpless* (*International Critical Commentary*, "Mark," Charles Scribner's Sons, 1896-1937, p. 294). This use of the verb would make it unnecessary to interpret the verse as the withdrawal of the divine presence. Gould takes the utterance as a query on Jesus' part as to why God had withheld divine help so that He, like the psalmist, had been delivered into the hands of His enemies. This interpretation understands the saying in a more natural way and does not create what must certainly be an insoluble mystery, that is, how God can desert Himself (in the form of the Son). It is the inaction of the Father in the face of such a cosmic tragedy, not His desertion, that leads Jesus to cry out, "My God, my God, why have you allowed me to be handed over to the enemy?"

Luke 2:52 says that Jesus increased in wisdom. If Jesus is God and God knows everything, how could there be anything for Jesus to learn?

That God is omniscient (all-knowing) is taught throughout Scripture.

It is equally clear in Scripture that Jesus is God. The angel appearing to Mary to announce the coming of the Christ child explained that the Holy Spirit would come upon her and that the child to be born would be called the Son of God (Luke 1:35). Throughout the fourth Gospel Jesus continually claimed a unique filial relationship with his heavenly Father (John 5:19; 6:38-40; 13:3; etc.). Paul calls him the "image of the invisible God" (Col. 1:15) and the author of Hebrews teaches that as Son, Jesus is the full and complete revelation of God (Heb. 1:1-2). Or, as John put it, no one but the only Son has ever seen God, and this One has made Him known (John 1:18).

It would seem to follow logically, then, that Jesus, being God, would share in His complete knowledge. And this would be true were it not for the necessary limitations of the incarnation. Some theologians have thought that Philippians 2:5ff. provides the clue. These verses teach that Jesus did not count equality with God a thing to be grasped, but emptied Himself, became a man and went all the way to the cross in His great act of humiliation. They interpret the *heauton ekenōsen* ("emptied Himself") as meaning that He emptied Himself of the independent exercise of His divine attributes. All the text says, however, is that He poured out or emptied *Himself*. Since Scripture does not attempt an explanation of the ontological changes involved in the second person of the eternal Godhead becoming man, it is best not to speculate. All we do know is that during the period of His incarnation Jesus increased in wisdom—which of course means that there were things that He did not know.

One of the more remarkable verses in the synoptic Gospels is Mark 13:32. There Jesus acknowledges, "But of that day or that hour no one knows, not even the angels in heaven, *nor the Son*, but only the Father" (italics mine). Not even towards the very end of His public ministry had the day or hour of the consummation of history been revealed to Him. The messianic role of Jesus required that He enter His own creation, take upon Himself the limitations of man, live victoriously without sin, and offer Himself as the infinite and perfect sacrifice to God the Father for the sins of man. This great achievement of Jesus the Christ necessitated the temporary cessation of His omniscience as God the eternal Son.

How He learned as a boy growing up in Nazareth one can only conjecture. I would think that in most areas of life He learned as would any other boy. At the proper age He learned to walk, and later to run. When He was old enough to help His father He learned the names of the carpenter's tools and how to choose the right wood for the right job. He undoubtedly learned vast portions of the Old Testament by memorization. Whether He always got 100 percent correct in arithmetic I haven't the faintest idea.

In addition to this kind of normal learning I would think that God gradually revealed to Him deep insights into Old Testament truth. At twelve years of age Jesus amazed the religious teachers at Passover with His understanding and answers (Luke 2:46-47). A dawning realization of His unique relationship with God is seen in His answer to His distraught parents, "Did you not know that I must be in my Father's house?"—or, "about my Father's business?" Although this statement makes it clear that Jesus was conscious of His unique relationship to God, many commentators believe that it was at His baptism that Jesus entered into the full realization that He was in fact the Son of God. The heavens opened and a voice declared, "This is my beloved Son" (Matt. 3:17). This interpretation is supported by the fact that within forty days the arch tempter twice attempted to drive a wedge of doubt into the self-consciousness of Jesus with the insidious "if you are the Son of God" (Matt. 4:3, 6).

Jesus may not have known the day of His return but He did know beyond doubt that

God was His Father in a unique sense and
that before Him lay a messianic ministry
which would lead ultimately to exaltation but
not before it had passed through the deep
valley of humiliation.

Just *before* **He died Jesus said, "It is
finished" (John 19:30). Since Jesus** *died*
**for our sins, how could His redemptive
work be finished** *before* **He died?**

It may be helpful to look at the synoptic accounts of the last moments of Jesus' life.
Matthew says that "Jesus cried again with a
loud voice and yielded up his spirit" (27:50).
Mark records the "loud cry" and adds that
He "breathed his last" (15:37). Luke gives us
the content of His final statement, "Father,
into thy hands I commit my spirit" (23:46).
By comparison, in the fourth Gospel we read
the famous utterance, "It is finished."
When we join these several accounts we arrive at a moving picture, not of a defeated
man whose life is being torn from Him, but
of victorious proclamation of a messianic mission carried triumphantly to its final conclusion. Alfred Loisy writes, "The death of the
Johannine Christ is not a scene of suffering,
of ignominy, of universal desolation . . . it is
the beginning of a great triumph" (cited by
Raymond Brown in *The Anchor Bible*, Double-
day, 1970).
What is it that was finished? The redemp-

tive task given by the Father and carried out victoriously by the Son. I Peter 3:18-20 teaches that subsequent to His death, Jesus then "went and preached to the spirits in prison." Commentators have always found this to be a difficult verse, but whatever it means it certainly does *not* say that Jesus had to suffer for the sins of man in hell. In other words, Jesus' payment for the sins of man was completed on the cross. When He cried "My God, my God, why hast thou forsaken me?" (Matt. 27:46; Mark 15:34) He was bearing our sins on the cross.

Therefore, it may rightly be said that Jesus "died spiritually" (that is, experienced separation from God the Father on our behalf—and this is the essence of spiritual death) *before* He died physically. The process, of course, led to the cessation of physical life in a short time.

If this explanation seems forced or unnatural, then it may be noted that two verses before Christ's physical death in the text of John says, "Jesus, knowing that all was now finished" (John 19:28). The same verb and verb tense is used in both verses, *tetelestai*. Perhaps Jesus is saying, by way of a slight temporal anticipation, I have completed my work on behalf of the redemption of man and with this next act of final surrender of my life it will all be over. In either case, however, the full payment for sin preceded whatever followed His last heartbeat. He did not suffer for sin after that moment.

Was it right for the eleven disciples to choose a replacement for Judas by casting lots? (Acts 1:26).

While this method has been questioned as rather unspiritual (G. Campbell Morgan believed that God intended Paul to be the twelfth disciple; *Acts of the Apostles*, Revell, 1924), it appears to have been practiced in biblical times with God's approval (cf. I Sam. 14:41). The Urim and Thummin were apparently two flat stones, light on one side and dark on the other, which the High Priest "rolled" in order to discern the will of God. Proverbs 16:3 says, "The lot is cast into the lap, but the decision is wholly from the Lord."

Even though the method may seem primitive to us today, could not have God, who controls all things, used even this practice to reveal His good pleasure?

Did Paul disobey God in continuing on to Jerusalem in spite of the prophet's warning? (Acts 21:10-15).

Returning from his third missionary journey Paul stayed a few days in Caesarea at the house of Philip the Evangelist. While there, a prophet named Agabus came down from Judea and acted out symbolically what would happen to Paul when he arrived in Jerusalem. Taking the apostle's belt he bound himself hand and foot declaring by the Holy Spirit that Paul would be similarly bound by the Jews in Jerusalem and delivered to the Gentiles. The apostle's friends urged him not to go but to no avail. He was willing not only to be bound but also to die for Christ (v. 13). Failing to dissuade him they said reluctantly, "The will of the Lord be done" (v. 14).

In this instance we appear to have an example of contradictory guidance. If Agabus spoke under inspiration of the Holy Spirit, how could it have been the Lord's will (cf. v. 14) for Paul to do the opposite? It should be noted, however, that Agabus does not tell Paul that it is against the will of God that he go to Jerusalem. His role was to point out in graphic fashion what would happen once the apostle got there. This would not come as a surprise to Paul because he had already told the Ephesian elders of the Spirit's revelation of coming trials (Acts 20:22-23).

Paul did not disobey God in going to Jerusalém. To the contrary, he went in obedience.

In all fairness we should call attention to the words of the disciples in Tyre (Acts 21:4) prior to Paul's stay in Caesarea. They indicate to Paul through the Spirit that he should not set foot in Jerusalem. This appears to be a clear directive not to proceed. But the words of the disciples at Tyre represent a telescoping of the prediction of Paul's fate and indicate the desire of the men of Tyre that the apostle not be "lost" to the cause of Christ. In other words, "This is what the Spirit has disclosed and we don't want you to walk straight into disaster."

The alternative to this interpretation would be that Paul disobeyed God and prematurely brought about his own removal from the Christian ministry. If this were true the Caesareans would have been wrong in concluding that for him to continue was the Lord's will (Acts 21:14).

4
Difficult Passages: Romans —Revelation

In Romans 7:14-25 is Paul describing his experience before or after conversion?

It seems to me that the text contains several strong indications that Paul is not referring to a preconversion spiritual struggle. In verse 22 he confesses that he delights in the law of God in his inmost self—hardly the testimony of one "dead in trespasses and sins." Further, at verse 14 Paul exchanges the past tense for the present and moves the discussion out of the category of past experience.

It would be equally wrong, however, to interpret Paul as describing a normal Christian experience. While there are struggles in the Christian life, the believer is certainly not sentenced to a life of continual frustration and endless defeat. To the question "Who will deliver me from this body of death? (v. 24) comes the answer. "Thanks be to God through Jesus Christ our Lord!" (v. 25). It is Christ who sets us free. In 8:2 Paul continues, "For the law of the Spirit of life in Christ Jesus [or "the law of the Spirit, that is, life in Christ Jesus" as A. M. Hunter has it]*has set me free* from the law of sin and death" (italics mine). How wrong to assume that the Christian must remain a helpless slave to the power of sin.

Although the literary form of this section is autobiographical, Paul is not describing a specific period in his life. The use of "I" is not by way of personal confession, but is a vivid way of getting the truth across. Paul is here sketching the struggle of the believer who at that particular moment is not appropriating the "law of the Spirit of life" for victory over the lingering presence of his old nature. It is neither preconversion nor normal Christian experience. It reflects a temporary failure to draw upon the source of all spiritual power.

In Romans 12:2 Paul writes that Christians are not to be conformed to this world. What is the "world" in the context of this verse?

The world is society organized and operating as if God were not around. When I was a boy, "worldliness" was rather neatly packaged and labeled so every good saint could avoid it. As I remember there were five basic sins—drinking, smoking, dancing, movies, and card playing.

Later on I learned that the list varies somewhat with regional views. It was T. W. Manson, a New Testament professor from England, who once suggested that the American church develop an "ethical atlas" for visiting preachers from abroad!

But worldliness is an attitude which lies much deeper than habits of life. This does not necessarily condone any of the above-mentioned practices but suggests a perspective which leads us to the heart of the problem. Lack of love is worldliness. Failure to be transformed in the inner man is worldliness. Materialism is worldliness. These and many others destroy the Christ-centered orientation of the believer's walk. While conduct is often a mirror of the inner man, that inner man will never be changed by altering the habits of his life. Jesus reminded his hearers that not to commit adultery is not enough—a man must not look lustfully at a woman (Matt. 5:27-28). Worldliness is a value structure which deceives man by encouraging him to live as though God were not around. The Christian, on the other hand, orients his entire existence around the active presence of God who is very much at work in this world.

Can Romans 14:5 be used to support not keeping the Sabbath?

Romans 14:5 reads, "One man esteems one day as better than another, while another man esteems all days alike." In the context the man who esteems one day as better is called the "weak man" (v. 2 by analogy). He is "weak" in the sense that he has been unable to overcome certain attitudes toward ceremonial taboos carried over from his pre-Christian religious life. Paul insists that the "stronger" should not despise the one who abstains and the "weaker" not pass judgment on the one who allows himself greater freedom (v. 3).

Now, how does this relate to Sunday? (I am taking "Sabbath" to mean the day of worship.) It would seem to me that if Sabbath-keeping were a part of the ceremonial legislation which gave way with the coming of Christ, Romans 14:5 would mean that it is perfectly permissible to treat Sunday like any other day—provided your conscience doesn't put up a fuss.

On the other hand, if the Sabbath is understood as giving expression to an eternal principle that man needs one day in seven to honor God and experience spiritual renewal by turning from his secular pursuits, the Romans verse is not applicable.

It is my opinion that the latter interpretation is correct. While we are not under law as a way of life, we certainly are obligated to those great eternal principles which found temporary expression in the historical development of the Old Testament. Thus the "all days" of Romans 14:5 is not intended as instruction about the day set aside for God but relates to ceremonial holy days of a specific pre-Christian period.

I Corinthians 13:10 says that when the perfect comes, the imperfect will pass away. Could the perfect be the New Testament and the imperfect speaking in tongues?

In verses 8-10 the apostle draws a comparison between love, which is permanent, and certain spiritual gifts, which are temporary. His purpose is to emphasize the superiority of love to those gifts which the Corinthians had elevated to such prominence.

Paul chooses three prominent gifts (prophecy, tongues, and knowledge) and demonstrates their transitory character. Both our knowledge and our prophesying are "in part" (*ek merous* stands in the emphatic position in both clauses). Our knowledge of truth is partial and our ability to communicate this truth is less than perfect. When that which is perfect has come, the imperfect will have run its course (*katargeō* in the passive means "to be rendered entirely idle").

Calvin wrote that "knowledge and prophecy

will therefore have a place in our lives, so long as imperfection clings to us, for they help us in our incompleteness" (*Commentary on First Corinthians*, Eerdmans).

The question is, What is *to telion* (the perfect)? Could it be the New Testament? One thing is certain—whatever it is, its coming marks the end of the partial. But since knowledge was not replaced by Scripture and since we still only partially understand what we shall some day fully comprehend, it follows that *to telion* has not yet come. Paul specifically says two verses later (13:12) that it is when we see face to face, that we shall fully understand. *To telion* carries with it the idea of a purpose or goal which has been determined. In this context it is God's end purpose towards which history is moving. Spiritual gifts help the church towards this goal but will no longer be necessary when the church stands face to face with its Redeemer. *To telion* is that final state of blessedness into which all Christians will be transformed at the coming of Christ (I John 3:2). At that point all that is imperfect shall fall away, but love will never end (v. 8). The lesson? Align the priorities of your life with that which abides.

Considering 1 Corinthians 14 (especially v. 39), would you say that tongues are out for this age?

Frankly, I Corinthians 14:39 seems to say that tongues are *in*! ("Do not forbid speaking in tongues.") At least in the early church if there were an interpreter present (v. 28), if each would wait his turn (vv. 29-33), if it could be carried on "decently and in order" (v. 40), and if it be kept in mind that five words of instruction are preferable to ten thousand words in a tongue (v. 19)—arithmetically that is two seconds of instruction against an hour of ecstasy—then Paul would say, "Go ahead."

Christians differ on whether the phenomenon of glossolalia was intended for the church universal throughout time. Advocates of the practice witness to its profoundly satisfying quality and the spiritual elevation it brings. Opponents point to a history of divisiveness and extremism which seems to have plagued the modern tongues movement.

That Paul valued instruction and evangelism over speaking in tongues is perfectly clear (14:19, 24). That he did not allow this preference to rule out tongues is also clear (14:39). Whether tongues are to play a meaningful role in the contemporary church is a question whose answer is necessarily dependent upon several larger considerations and therefore calls for a tentative expression of opinion in humility and love.

In I Corinthians 14:17 Paul seems to have a low view of baptism. How do you explain this?

The two statements which occasion this question are probably, "I am thankful that I baptized none of you" (v. 14) and "Christ did not send me to baptize but to preach the gospel" (v. 17). Admittedly these verses are a bit awkward for those groups that emphasize the significance of baptism.

Preparing to answer this question I checked through an unabridged concordance to locate all the verses in Paul's letters which treat the subject of baptism. I was surprised to find that apart from the paragraph in I Corinthians 1, Christian baptism is mentioned in only five places. These five verses say essentially three things: 1) The believer is baptized into the death of Christ (Rom. 6:3f.). 2) He is raised to new life with Christ (Gal. 3:27; Col. 2:12). 3) This results in a unity of all believers (I Cor. 12:13; Eph. 4:5).

The truth set forth by these verses is important. Our union with Christ in His death is a farewell to the old life centered in self and lived out for personal advantage. Our union with Christ in His resurrection supplies the power to walk in newness of life. By one Spirit we have been baptized into one body and all artificial barriers, social and ethnic, have fallen away. While these truths permeate New Testament teaching, the figure of baptism by which they are so aptly portrayed is not often used.

To return to your question—it is my opinion that Paul was infinitely more concerned with the inner transformation of which baptism was a figure than with the external ritual through which it was given expression in the early church. Christians who understand baptism in a more sacramental way will differ with me at this point. It does, however, explain Paul's attitude in I Corinthians 1 where partisanship (encouraged to some degree by baptismal practice) was jeopardizing Christian unity.

This does not, however, represent a "low view of baptism." That rite which gave expression to the most marvelous and transforming experience of life was by no means available on a take-it-or-leave-it basis in the early Church. I believe that Paul had a "high view of baptism," not because the rite possessed some magical efficacy but because of the great truth it symbolized.

How literally should Christians take II Corinthians 6:17, "Therefore come out from them, and be separate from them, says the Lord"?

In an earlier letter Paul had corrected the

Corinthians' misunderstanding about his instructions regarding association with immoral men. He had in mind those claiming to be Christians, not the immoral of this world, "since then [they] would need to go out of the world" (I Cor. 5:9-10). In response, it seems that they had interpreted this as an apostolic okay for rather extensive and permanent relationships between themselves and the pagan society in which they lived.

Such a relationship, Paul now says, would be entirely out of place because of totally different standards of righteousness and moral rectitude. Believers have come out of darkness into light. There is no working agreement between Christ and Satan. God's temple has nothing in common with heathen idolatry. And believers are God's temple. Drawing upon a chain of Old Testament texts Paul calls them *from* the world and its wickedness into a family relationship with God who is holy and righteous. As the children of Israel left behind in Babylon all that was unclean (II Cor. 6:17 quoting Isa. 52:11), so are they to cleanse themselves from every defilement (II Cor. 7:1) and be received into the fellowship of God's holy family.

The real separation Paul has in mind is separation from sin. To what extent this is encouraged by loosening ties with the non-Christian world is another, but related, question. To be "unequally yoked" (KJV; or "mismated," RSV) with unbelievers means to compromise with them (cf. *Tyndale New Testament Commentaries*, "II Corinthians," Eerdmans, 1957-71, p. 98) rather than to marry them, although the latter would undoubtedly involve the former. Each Christian is under obligation to separate himself from sin. To what extent this will involve separation from unbelievers will have to be worked out by every Christian in the total context of his daily life and ministry.

In reading Ephesians I noticed that Paul used the word *mystery* **six times and each time somewhat differently. I'm confused!**

Apart from a single statement of Jesus which is recorded in all three of the synoptic Gospels and four occurrences of the word in Revelation, the term "mystery" is found exclusively in the New Testament within the Pauline writings (twenty-one times). A quick survey of Paul's letters shows that he speaks of the "myteries of God" (I Cor. 4:1), the mystery of [God's] will" (Eph. 1:9), the "mystery of lawlessness" (II Thess. 2:7), the "mystery of the faith" (I Tim. 3:9), and the "mystery of our religion" (I Tim. 3:16).

In classical Greek the word *mustērion* (mystery) referred to anything which was hidden or secret. But in the New Testament a *mustērion* is something *formerly* unknown by man but *now* made plain by divine revelation. The typical Pauline usage is quite clear in a passage such as Ephesians 3:4-5, where the apostle speaks of "the mystery of Christ, which was not made known to the sons of men in other generations as it has now been revealed to his holy apostles and prophets by the Spirit." Since the New Testament is the fulfillment in Christ of God's promises in the Old Testament, we would expect it to be a book of revelation, not a book of secrets. That which was obscure to the prophets of the old dispensation is now open and clear to those who follow after the event. We might even say that the word "mystery" is a theological anacronism which reflects the progressive nature of divine revelation.

Please explain Ephesians 4:26, "Be angry but do not sin; do not let the sun go down on your anger."

Ephesians 4:26 stands alone in the New Testament in teaching that anger (of some sort) has a place in the life of the Christian. Before attempting an interpretation of this particular verse I would like to look elsewhere in Scripture to see what God has to say about anger.

In the Sermon on the Mount, Jesus said that "every one who is angry with his brother shall be liable to judgment" (Matt. 5:22). The King James follows an inferior text in reading "angry without a cause." Knowing that every angry man believes he has a reason to be angry, Jesus allows no exceptions. Turning to the apostle Paul we find that he lists anger along with such other sins as strife, jealousy, dissension, and drunkenness as works of the flesh (Gal. 5:20). They rise from the unregenerate nature of man and stand in vivid contrast to such fruit of the Spirit as love, joy, and peace (cf. Gal. 5:22).

In Ephesians 4:31-32 Paul admonishes believers to put away all wrath and anger and instead "be kind to one another, tenderhearted, forgiving one another, as God in Christ forgave you." This is so important that he repeats it again in Colossians 3:8.

Near the end of his life Paul once again wrote, "I desire then that in every place the men should pray, lifting holy hands without anger . . ." (I Tim. 2:8). There is something essentially incongruous between holiness and human anger.

The only other reference to anger in the life of a Christian is found in James. There the brother of our Lord wrote, "Let every man be quick to hear, slow to speak, slow to anger, for the anger of man does not work the righteousness of God" (James 1:19, 20). How many of us would have to confess that slow to hear, quick to speak, and instantly angry is pretty much the story of our life?

This brief survey should indicate that anger in the normal sense of the word has absolutely no place in a believer's life. Anger is a destructive force which leaves in its wake broken relationships and irreparable personal damage.

How then shall we understand Paul's instructions, "Be angry but do not sin"? A look at the Greek offers little help. The imperative, *orgidzesthe*, is simply a verb form of the noun *orgē*, the common word for anger found throughout the New Testament. The noun *thumos* (wrath) is essentially synonymous but somewhat more appropriate where an outburst of rage is envisioned. (The breathy quality of the word in Greek betrays its origin as passion.)

A clue may be found in the fact that *orgē* is used at least thirty times in the New Testament in connection with the anger or wrath of God. When speaking of God as angry we must adjust our terminology to what we know of the nature of God. The "anger" of God is His divine reaction to evil. It has nothing to do with the uncontrolled outbursts of emotion which are characteristic of human anger. God's anger is moral indignation, a necessary response of His righteousness. For example, Paul speaks of "immorality, impurity, passion, evil desire, and covetousness" as supplying the reason why "the wrath of God is coming" (Col. 3:5).

It appears then that we must distinguish between anger as a sinful expression of the unregenerate nature and anger as moral indignation. It is in this latter sense that the apostle said, "Be angry." There is a place for the believer to react with righteous abhorrence to the sudden spectacle of evil and degradation. But be careful! In the same breath Paul adds, "but do not sin." Human nature is such that it cannot sustain for any length of time this divine reaction of righteous indignation. So the apostle adds, "The sunset must not find you still angry" (Knox).

What does it mean to grieve the Holy Spirit? (Eph. 4:30)

The teaching of Scripture is that the Holy Spirit is a person. As a person He possesses those attributes which are essential to human existence as we know it. Thus He thinks, feels, wills. Even when we have acknowledged a high degree of anthropomorphism in such statements we must still agree that He does in fact think, feel, and will. As His thinking is higher than ours and His willing encounters no inner opposition, so also are His emotions different from ours in that they are untainted with the results of estrangement from God.

To grieve the Holy Spirit is to cause Him sorrow. It is to press ahead in the act of disobedience despite the warning which He raises within our consciousness. It is this overriding of the voice of God and continuing in an act of willful sin that grieves the Holy Spirit.

The context of the admonition in Ephesians 4 is illuminating. In the verse immediately preceding Paul had written, "Let no evil talk come out of your mouths, but only such as is good for edifying," and in the verse following he instructs the Ephesians to put away bitterness, wrath, anger, clamor, and *slander* (v. 31). Could it be that we grieve the Holy Spirit primarily by the words which come from our mouths? Perhaps this is, after all, the supreme test of our sensitivity to spiritual things. The gift of speech has allowed man to develop and transmit a culture, to maintain communication with his peers, and to lift his voice in praise of God who made it all possible. How perverse if he should place it at the disposal of the adversary!

Explain Philippians 2:12: "Work out your own salvation with fear and trembling."

Here is another place where the believer's soteriological concern has led to some fancy exegetical footwork. The "salvation" to which Paul refers is deliverance from the threat of disunity which was beginning to rear its ugly head at Philippi. Earlier in the chapter he felt obliged to counsel them to "count others better than yourselves" (v. 3). Later in the letter he tells the church that Euodia and Syntyche—or as someone has translated, "You, Odious, and Soon Touchy"—are "to agree in the Lord" (4:2). The church is to work out its problems, with their real and ominous potential for disunity, in fear and trembling because it is God Himself who is there at work in the midst of their assembly.

The word *sōtēria* (salvation) does not necessarily denote eternal salvation. This can be seen in its earlier usage in Philippians 1:19. There Paul speaks of his experience of imprisonment which shall turn out to his "salvation." Most scholars regard release from jail as the intention of the phrase.

In regard to the uses of "salvation" here and in I Timothy 2:15, it is interesting to read Barclay's discussion of the term in *Jesus As They Saw Him* (Harper and Row, 1963). He discusses eight different meanings which can be seen in the Greek Old Testament. The first is simply *peace or welfare* (Gen. 26:31). Isaiah uses it to mean preservation in safety (Isa. 12:2). Particularly relevant is Hannah's rejoicing in her "salvation" (I Sam. 2:1) or her deliverance from the unhappy situation of being childless. Other meanings include help, assistance and deliverance (I Sam. 11:9); deliverance and victory combined (I Sam. 23:11; II Sam. 19:2; I Chron. 11:14); rescue in danger (Exod. 14:13); rescue from sin (Ps. 51:14), and eschatological deliverance (Isa. 49:6; 52:10).

Colossians 1:15 speaks of Christ as "the firstborn of every creature" (KJV). Doesn't this seem to support the claim that Christ is less than God?

It is interesting that this phrase is taken out of what is probably the most exalted christological passage in the entire New Testament. Colossians 1:15-20 tells us that Christ is the image of the invisible God (v. 15), and by Him, through Him (*di' autou*), and for Him all things were created (v. 16), and in Him all fulness dwells (v. 19; cf. 2:9).

The significance of "firstborn" is not temporal: it expresses preeminence. Christ is not the first of a series of created beings. Rather, "all things were created by him . . . and he is before all things" (vv. 16b-17a, KJV). Scripture teaches that Christ has existed eternally as the second person of the Trinity. He is the eternal Son of God. It was at the incarnation that He became, in a sense, a part of His own creation. From that point on He is the God-man. The heresy that Jesus Christ is somehow less than God is a misinterpretation of Scripture which goes back to what was one of the earliest controversies of the postapostolic church.

Explain in what way Paul's suffering "complete[s] what is lacking in Christ's afflictions" (Col. 1:24).

On the surface this much disputed verse seems to say that Paul's sufferings were a necessary supplement to Christ's sufferings on the cross. But such an idea runs counter to a basic conviction of the apostle that the death of Jesus was a once-for-all event through which complete salvation is extended to man. To suggest that believers shared in the atoning work of Christ would have been branded as rank heresy by the early church.

It should be noted that the word "afflictions" in this passage (*thlipseōn*) is never used for the actual sufferings of Jesus on the cross or during His ministry (C. F. D. Moule, *Cambridge Greek Testament Commentary*, Cambridge.

Some writers take the verse as a reference to the idea of a quota of suffering which the Christian community must undergo before God's purposes will be complete. Mark 13:8 (and parallels) speaks of wars, earthquakes and famines as "the beginning of the sufferings" which leads into great tribulation (*thlipsis*, v. 19) and the return of the Son of Man (v. 26). Luke 21:24 designates a specific time period for this tribulation ("until the times of the Gentiles are fulfilled"). This predestinarian concept is found elsewhere in the New Testament as well (cf. Rom. 11:25; I Thess. 2:16; Heb. 11:40; Rev. 6:11).

It is more likely, however, that Paul was thinking of the sufferings which were bound to come his way as he carried out his ministry on behalf of the body of Christ, the church. On the Damascus road he learned that in persecuting the Christian church, he was persecuting Jesus (Acts 9:4-5). He was soon to learn from Ananias "how much he must suffer for the sake of [Christ's] name" (Acts 9:16).

To suffer for Christ is to complete or fill out what yet remains of the afflictions which are inevitably involved in the growth and ministry of the church. Paul rejoiced in the opportunity to repay somewhat in kind his debt to Christ who suffered for him and in so doing to hasten the end of all sorrow and suffering at the return of Christ.

Since the Bible says that "bodily exercise profiteth little" (I Tim. 4:8, KJV), why do Christians get so involved in sports activities?

"Bodily exercise profiteth little" *appears* to suggest that it is of little use to become involved in any program of regular physical exercise. Jogging, or whatever, is essentially a waste of time. But does Paul *mean* that? A quick survey of several modern speech translations suggests that the apostle is not putting down physical fitness. The Revised Standard Version says, "Bodily training is of some value," and Williams writes, "Physical training, indeed, is of some service." Who is right? To answer this requires a look at the slightly larger context.

A composite paraphrase of I Timothy 4:7-8 could read as follows: "As for profane legends and old wives' tales, leave them alone (The Twentieth Century New Testament). Spend your time and energy in the exercise of keeping spiritually fit (Living Letters). Bodily fitness has a certain value but spiritual fitness is essential (Phillips) since it carries with it a promise of life, both here and hereafter" (Montgomery). The issue is not whether physical exercise is of value but whether spiritual fitness is of *supreme* value. The argument is that of the lesser to the greater.

If you accept the premise that spiritual fitness is of greater ultimate significance than physical fitness, and in fact you do involve yourself in a program of sorts which leads to a strong and healthy physique, then how much more should you enter into a program of training in godliness which will result in a healthy spiritual condition! Especially since its benefits go beyond this life into the next.

Let me put the issue in a different way. Hockey is a tremendously exciting game. From the first face-off until the final siren it is packed full of dramatic spine-tingling action. It is no game for anyone who will not give it everything he's got. The goalie is called on to withstand two hundred pounds of coordinated muscle as it bears down with lightning speed to drive the puck toward his goal at speeds in excess of 100 miles per hour.

Have you ever watched a good collegiate wrestling match? Have you seen the tremendous exertion of a man who, having lost the advantage, is barely keeping his shoulders off the mat? Here is a sport that calls for strength, balance, timing, coordination, and cunning. A good wrestler is the product of countless hours of rigorous training and constant self-discipline. It is a sport only for the man who is prepared to give everything he has for a long time.

Why do I talk about hockey and wrestling? Simply because of the shocking disparity between the determination of the athlete and what often passes for Christian commitment. Should not the disciple of Jesus Christ throw himself into the pursuit for holiness with the same abandon that the young man gives himself to physical conditioning? Should not our motivation to serve Christ be as strong as our desire to throw a ball through a basket or to slide down a snowy slope on two sticks of wood?

I'm 100 percent for athletics. I believe in maintaining the body which God has given us in top physical condition. I fully appreciate the value of competition. But what's wrong with approaching the Christian life with the same vigorous determination? Paul's favorite metaphors were taken from the athletic games and military life. Is he not saying that in the Christian race there is room only for those who joyfully give themselves to life's challenge with all the concentrated effort of an athlete bent hard on winning? "So run that you may obtain [the prize]"! (I Cor. 9:24b).

Does I Timothy 5:23 ("Use a little wine for the sake of your stomach and your frequent ailments") condone the use of alcoholic beverages?

If you are asking whether Paul's advice on this particular occasion in about A.D. 64 is biblical precedent for the indiscriminate use of both wine and hard liquor in the twentieth century, the answer is no. Such an interpretation would ignore the rules of general semantics, illogically generalize from a particular instance, and blandly assume that today's bleary-eyed inebriate behind the wheel of a two-hundred horsepower instrument of destruction is no greater threat to society than was a drunken camel driver in the first century.

That the "wine" of I Timothy 5 was a drink which, if taken in excess, could lead to drunkenness follows from the fact that it is the same Greek word (*oinos*) which is used in Ephesians 5:18, "Do not get drunk with wine." This Greek word and the Hebrew equivalent (*yayin*) occur more than 170 times in the Bible and generally refer to the fermented juice of the grape. It is the wine of Genesis 9:21 on which Noah became drunk after the flood. (For an excellent article on the subject, read, "Wine Drinking in New Testament Times" by Robert H. Stein, *Christianity Today,* June 20, 1975, pp. 9–11.)

In the case of Timothy, one observation needs to be clearly made: the use of wine was for medical purposes. It would appear that Timothy was of a retiring nature. Paul had to admonish him to correct the false doctrine (I Tim. 1:3-4) and urge him not to be reticent because of his youth (I Tim 4:11-12). In his desire not to be a stumbling block Timothy had taken to heart Paul's prior advice in Romans 14:21, "It is right not to eat meat or drink wine or do anything that makes your brother stumble." But at the point where such abstinence was a threat to his health, Paul now advises a little wine for medicinal purposes.

Does II Timothy 2:15 teach the dispensational approach to Bible study?

In the King James Version the verse reads, "Study to shew theyself approved unto God, a workman that needeth not to be ashamed, *rightly dividing the word of truth*" (italics mine).

It is this final phrase which has often been used to support the idea that proper interpretation of Scripture demands that time be divided into a definite sequence of dispensations on the basis of God's various ways of dealing with man. The crucial question is: Does this interpretive approach arise from the verse itself or has it been attached to the verse because the English translation of the participle (*orthotomounta*, "rightly dividing") opens the door to misunderstanding?

The first phrase would be better translated, "Strive to present yourself *approved* unto God." In contrast with those who dispute about words (v. 14), Timothy is to present himself as an unashamed workman. Divine approval is to be gained by "rightly dividing the word of truth." Proper interpretation of the verse hinges on a correct understanding of the Greek verb underlying the participle.

Originally the verb (which occurs only here in the New Testament) meant "to cut straight" and was probably drawn from the tailor cutting fabric according to a pattern. If the word as Paul used it still retained this original vividness, the phrase would mean by analogy that Christian truth should be expounded according to its proper pattern— that provided by the gospel.

It is more probable, however, that the metaphor has faded and come to mean "to manage rightly" (cf. ASV, "handling aright"). Instead of wasting time in argumentation (v. 14) and word battles (v. 16), Timothy was to handle the Word of Truth in a straightforward manner. The New English Bible translates it, "driving a straight furrow, in your proclamation of the truth."

Interpreted in context, the verse has nothing to do with studying Scripture with careful attention to a prescribed series of dispensations.

Does Hebrews 10:14 teach Christian perfection?

Hebrews 10:14 reads, "For by a single offering he has perfected for all time those who are sanctified." The perfection spoken of here is what may be called convenantal perfection. The old Mosaic system failed to bring people the full assurance of forgiveness of sins and fellowship with God (cf. Heb. 10:1-4). The new convenant established by Christ's single sacrifice of Himself has made this new and living relationship possible. This perfection of fellowship involves forgiveness of sin (vv. 17-18) and confidence to stand in the presence of God (vv. 19-22). In this sense every believer is perfect.

Convenantal perfection, however, does not imply sinlessness. John leaves no doubt about this when he categorically affirms, "If we say we have no sin, we deceive ourselves, and the truth is not in us" (I John 1:8). "Becoming what we are" is the whole story of sanctification. Transformed by grace as a result of faith, the course of the believer's life is away from the dominion of sin into an ever-increasing likeness to Jesus Christ.

What does James 5:19-20 mean where it talks about converting a brother who has erred from the truth and in this way saving his soul from death?

Although these two verses are rather obscure, several points are clear: the man in question is a Christian brother; he has wandered from the truth; he is designated a sinner. The problem that lurks behind the verse is the implication that persistence in (theological) error results in death (loss of salvation?).

One answer (which doesn't satisfy the full expression, "shall save his soul from death") is that the early church believed that continuance in sin could result in physical death. Did not Paul say in I Corinthians 11:30 that lack of discernment in taking communion explained why "many of you are weak and ill, and some have died"?

A preferable answer is composed of the following observations:

1. The situation is described within a conditional framework: "If any of you do err." This stops short of a direct affirmation that some in fact do.

2. The situation is not one in which a believer has already lost his salvation, but one in which an erring Christian who has

wandered from the truth stands in jeopardy.

3. The verb "convert" in this context does not mean "accept Christ as Savior," but "bring back to the truth" (cf. Peter's "conversion" in Luke 22:32).

The larger context throws an interesting light on the problem. James has just been speaking of the tremendous power of prevailing prayer. By prayer the sick are healed, sinners are forgiven, and rain from heaven is stopped. Does this not suggest that prayer is also a proper way to bring back to the truth those who have wandered into error? In our day when the mass media are so often used by religious broadcasters to correct one another's "heresy," how refreshing it would be if the critics were first to subject their evaluations to the acid test of sincere prayer.

Who are the twenty-four elders of Revelation 4?

The majority of commentators who write on a popular level have identified the twenty-four elders as a heavenly priesthood (cf. I Chron. 24) representing the Old Testament saints and the church of the present age. Their garments of white are said to speak of the righteousness of Christ and their golden crowns of the rewards promised in verses such as II Timothy 4:7-8. The basic reason for this identification is their song of praise in chapter five: "Thou ... hast redeemed us to God by thy blood ... and hast made *us* ... kings and priests: and *we* shall reign on the earth" (vv. 9-10, KJV,) (italics mine). Hence it appears that the twenty-four elders represent the total number of the redeemed.

Unfortunately the verse as it is rendered in the King James Version is based upon a series of interior readings. The better Greek manuscripts omit the first "us" and read "them" and "they" for the two other pronouns. This definitely distinguishes the twenty-four elders from those who have been redeemed. Most New Testament scholars hold the elders to be an exalted order of angelic beings. They are part of the heavenly throne-room scene and add their praise to that of the four living creatures, the angels, and all creation.

5
God and the Contemporary Scene

For a number of people, the word *theology* has an ominous sound. It connotes learned divines discussing great and complex metaphysical issues in the candle-lit rooms of medieval monasteries. More accurately, it is the study of God and His relations with the universe. In a secondary sense it designates the study of religious doctrines.

The discussions which follow are theological only in a broad and general way. They rise very naturally out of a common desire to gain a better understanding of some basic and perplexing issues. Professional theologians may feel that simple answers are less than satisfactory (and in many cases they are right). Some issues, however, are not necessarily distorted by the simple answer. While it is important to understand that metaphysical questions are infinitely complex it does not follow that simple answers may not be functionally appropriate.

We may as well start with a question that has been asked since the beginning of time.

Is it possible to prove the reality of God?

God does not submit Himself to empirical verification for the benefit of a man who is not satisfied with the inner assurances of faith. Rather He graciously makes Himself known to those who approach Him openly as a person.

While study of the intricacies of existence ought to lead man toward belief, all too often it leads in the opposite direction. The scientific method, which has done so much for the material progress of Western civilization, is inappropriate when applied to the domain of metaphysics. The Russian cosmonaut who failed to find God in his initial orbit around the earth is a painful example of the self-hypnotic influence of scientism.

Jesus said, "If a man loves me, he will keep my word, and my Father will love him, and we will come to him and make our home with him" (John 14:23). The abiding presence of God in the life of a believer is all the "proof" needed of His reality.

The erosion of confidence often results more from a break in meaningful fellowship than from any logical conclusion which can be drawn from the relevant data. I am reminded of a friend's observation that "the things we tend to think about most are the things which seem most real."

Is God the father of all men or of believers only?

In the first decade of the twentieth century, theological liberalism was front and center on the ideological stage. Most of its represent-atives confidently asserted that Jesus propounded a doctrine of "the fatherhood of God and the brotherhood of man." This was interpreted to mean that no longer would it be possible or necessary to separate the human family into categories of "lost" and "saved." Some may not have yet entered fully into their inheritance but all sustain the same basic relationship to a benevolent heavenly Father. Earthly fathers seldom disenfranchise their children; the heavenly Father never would. In its popular form this pleasant doc-trine was warmly received by a self-indulgent Christendom.

But is it biblical? As always, this is the crucial question.

Turning to Scripture we find, in the first place, that in a general sense it is true that God as Creator sustains a certain fatherly relationship to the world at large. Paul, in Athens, declared, "In him [God] we live and move and have our being; as even some of your poets have said, 'For we are indeed his offspring' " (Acts 17:28).

In the Old Testament we find God portrayed as the Father of the nation Israel. Moses is told to declare unto Pharaoh, "Thus says the Lord, Israel is my first-born son, and I say to you, 'Let my son go that he may serve me'" (Exod. 4:22-23).

Thus the way is prepared for the New Testament teaching that although man was created by natural affinity for sonship to God, sin intervened and frustrated his true destiny. This destiny can now be restored only through the new birth. John stoutly declares that it is to those who receive Him, who believe in His name, that He gives power to become children of God.

The sonship that issues in eternal life is not *natural man's* relationship to God as *Creator*. It is, rather, *redeemed man's* relationship to God as *Savior*. In confusing fatherhood by creation with fatherhood by re-creation, theological liberalism turned a blind eye to the basic problem of human existence—the problem of sin.

Only those who bear a moral resemblance to their heavenly Father as a result of the new birth and a continuing growth in grace can rightly be called "sons of God."

If God made us for fellowship with Himself, why is communication so indirect and abstruse?

In the August 1973 issue of *Eternity* I

argued that the believer can know the will of God. This question is a variation on the same theme. I would contend that, as a general rule, God's communication with man is neither indirect nor abstruse. "Indirect" suggests that God is not immediately available for consultation and "abstruse" implies that when He does speak His words are too difficult to fully comprehend.

Neither claim is consistent with the New Testament teaching of God's great act of self-revelation in the incarnation of Jesus Christ His Son. Hebrews begins with the declaration that following the intermittent and partial revelations of God in times past, there was provided in Christ the ultimate revelation—that of a perfect Son who reflects the glory of His Father and bears the very stamp of His nature (Heb. 1:3). This complete and totally accurate expression of the nature and will of God leaves nothing unsaid that needs to be known by man.

"But that is all theology," you say. "In my prayers I can't seem to get through. I don't understand why life fell apart in my hands. Why is not God present when I need Him most?"

The answer is that God *is* present. He may not function like a fortune-telling machine that pops out a little card giving weight and fortune whenever it is fed a penny, but He is nevertheless present. (If He is not there He is nowhere, because God as spirit has no spatial limitations.) It may be that He has decided to remain quiet for a while out of a profound respect for your ability to consider again the question and find the answer on your own. How will Christian maturity ever be reached if we insist on receiving from God ready-made answers to all of life's complex problems? God has endowed us with both reason and "sanctified common sense" to manage much of life's normal operations. It is proper for a father to support his six-year-old son as he tries for the first time to ride a new bicycle. But not when the son is twenty!

Chapter twelve of Hebrews may be helpful at this point. "My son, do not regard lightly the discipline of the Lord, nor lose courage when you are punished by him. For the Lord disciplines him whom he loves, and chastises every son whom he receives. . . . For the moment all discipline seems painful rather than pleasant; later it yields the peaceful fruit of righteousness to those who have been trained by it" (Heb. 12:5b-6, 11). *Paideia*, discipline, means upbringing, training, instruction. As master teacher, God will speak when the time is right. His silence for the moment indicates that you are still learning. Because God is all-wise, He knows exactly what circumstances are necessary for your maximum growth in Christian character. Your part is to believe and wait patiently.

How good are the times of refreshing

which stem from conscious active fellowship with God! Over the span of a believer's life these happy times are certainly the norm. The promise stands, "Draw near to God and he will draw near to you" (James 4:8). Even when He is silent He is nevertheless near. A loving heavenly Father does not communicate indirectly and abstrusely with His struggling children. In Christ He has spoken definitively and finally. In the circumstances of life He speaks as friend to friend. Occasional moments of silence occur only when to speak would retard growth toward spiritual maturity.

If freedom is to be measured in terms of available alternatives, isn't obedience to God a form of bondage?

To the nonbeliever, the Christian life appears to be a series of restrictions on personal freedom. Christians are often caricatured as rather lifeless individuals who have surrendered everything that is really appealing and have settled for a negative existence which is no more than bondage to a heavenly tyrant.

In the sixth chapter of Romans, Paul asks, "Do you not know that if you yield yourselves, to any one as obedient slaves, you are slaves of the one whom you obey, either of sin, which leads to death, or of obedience, which leads to righteousness?" (Rom. 6:16;

cf. vv. 12-23 for the larger context). Apparently, man may choose between two types of slavery; slavery to sin or slavery to God.

It is clear, however, that the apostle expects his readers to recognize that he is using the term "slave" equivocally, that is, in a way that allows some variation in application. Slavery to God and slavery to sin are alike only in the sense of involving total allegiance which results in complete control. The connotations attached to slavery to sin (heartache, sorrow, remorse) cannot be transferred to the idea of slavery as applied to God.

Nevertheless, if freedom may be defined as having available the maximum number of alternatives, doesn't it follow that obedience to God reduces these alternatives and consequently makes a person less free?

We could turn to John 8:36 and read, "If the Son makes you free, you will be free indeed"—and this is a definitive answer—but it may be helpful to probe a bit to discover just how obedience increases one's alternatives rather than reducing them. Let's put the issue into a couple of specific settings.

Consider the man who through excessive and compulsive drinking has become an alcoholic. He is a slave, bound to his habit. He has sacrificed home, family, job, and friends in order to do the bidding of his new master. This man has very few real alternatives. He can no longer choose a vacation with his family because they are lost to him and he has nothing left to provide for such an occasion. He can no longer accept a promotion in his firm because he has no job. Bondage to sin (and remember, the invitation to take the first drink was an appeal to exercise freedom) has drastically reduced his viable alternatives.

In this case, obedience to God would obviously have expanded his alternatives. He would have been free to enjoy his family, choose vacations, find satisfaction in responsible work, etc. A clear mind would have provided the opportunity to think clearly and an effective life would have presented the alternative to use his influence for the good. In the representative case of the alcoholic, obedience to God cannot be conceived of as a limiting factor or a curtailment of freedom. On the contrary, obedience would have provided the gateway to increased freedom.

Or take a self-centered person. To the extent that he uses "freedom" as an occasion to promote his own selfish desires he forges the chains of his own slavery. In time, isolated selfish acts will harden into disregard for others and fixation upon personal advantage. In this way self-centeredness robs a person of the ability to build lasting friendships and to enjoy the appreciation of others. Slavery to self *reduces*, not expands, a person's alternatives.

It all boils down to this: sin is bondage and obedience is freedom. The apparent restrictions involved in obedience are in truth the signposts that indicate the path to maximum freedom. Satan calls attention to the limitations required by obedience and would have the unwary believe that God's way leads into the dead end of a restricted existence. But then, he has always been the "deceiver of the whole world" (Rev. 12:9) and we ought to be able to recognize his devious ways by now!

Think of God's will as revealed in Scripture as His gracious way of guiding you past the enticements laid by Satan (which would rob you of freedom) and into a life of ever-increasing joy and maximum opportunity to become exactly what you will want to be when you stand in His presence.

As George Matheson, the blind poet-preacher of Edinburgh, put it, "Make me a captive, Lord, and then I shall be free. Force me to render up my sword, and I shall conqueror be."

Since man is a free moral agent, on what basis can the church, society, or even God, impose upon him an external code of conduct?

Basic to this question is the nature of freedom. Some think of freedom as the inalienable right to do whatever one wants to do. A moment's reflection will show that in a normal society no one actually regulates his conduct by any such idea of freedom. We live by the laws of the land, respect the rights of our neighbors, and try not to violate city ordinances. In this we are not relinquishing freedom but defining it in terms of the rights of others.

Hence freedom may be defined as the opportunity to do that which is for the ultimate good. There is no such thing as freedom to injure another. Since freedom is a social matter it must involve some sort of social regulation. We slow to thirty-five miles per hour in a Thirty-five-miles-per-hour zone, not with bitterness that our freedom has been curtailed, but as evidence that we are willing to observe the rights of the pedestrian. A Christian accepts the will of God as the proper boundaries within which to enjoy his rights as a free moral agent. To transgress is not to exercise freedom but to demonstrate irresponsibility. The idea of unrestricted personal conduct which acknowledges neither the sovereignty of God nor the moral consciousness of an enlightened society is not freedom but anarchy.

What has happened to the "God is dead" theology we heard so much about a few years ago?

I personally do not believe that the "God is dead" movement is dead. The phrase itself helped thrust the idea into public view before there was an adequate market for the ideology. Like a brilliant comet it blazed across the theological sky—but there the analogy stops. Madison Avenue may have decided to switch its energies to other promising spectaculars, but the basic idea of a non-supernatural world view is still growing. Secularism has plagued the people of God since the beginning. It is the supreme enemy of all who place their faith in a transcendent God. The dramatic rise of technology in the West unconsciously influences modern man to believe in what he can see and what he can do. A humble commitment to suprasensible reality and the vastness of that which man cannot know or cannot do on his own is increasingly rare in a progress-oriented society.

"God is dead" theology may change its name to something a bit less spectacular, but it will not go away. Ultimately it finds expression in the beast of Revelation who locks in mortal combat with the forces of righteousness. When this happens, all the world will most certainly know that God is not dead!

Are writers serious when they speak of modern times as the post-Christian era?

Yes. A rather large number of contemporary theologians believe that Christianity in its institutionalized form—complete with time-honored ritual and inflexible dogma—is a thing of the past. "Man come of age" is Bonhoeffer's phrase and is used to symbolize an understanding of God as having brought man to maturity and then stepping back into the shadows. Man is on his own, and now, like Jesus, is to become a "man for others."

However courageous this theological stance, it bears no resemblance to the biblical portrayal. Jesus said, "If a man loves me, he will keep my word, and my Father will love him, and *we will come to him and make our home with him*" (John 14:23, italics mine). No *Deus in absentia* here!

Paul added, "It is no longer I who live, but Christ who lives in me" (Gal. 2:20). While it may be true that last century's liturgy is giving way to this century's informality, the heart of the Christian faith will always be the risen and reigning Lord Jesus Christ, ever present with those who believe.

What does Bonhoeffer mean by "religionless Christianity"?

One of the most influential theological thinkers of recent years has been Dietrich Bonhoeffer who, at the age of thirty-nine (in 1945), was put to death in a Gestapo prison. Many of his phrases have become part of today's theological vocabulary. Bonhoeffer felt that man was moving toward a time when he would no longer require God as a "working hypothesis." Previously, preaching had counted upon the fact that, down deep, man had felt a need for God. However in the past one hundred years or so man has gained a self-assurance making him willing to carry on without God. He feels that not only is the divine being unnecessary in the everyday affairs of life, but also in the more ultimate questions of guilt and death. Bonhoeffer's position is that God in the twentieth century is calling us to a new form of Christianity which has nothing to do with the religious premise. This "religionless Christianity" is not simply Christianity without ritual. It is Christianity without any dependence upon an inner need. God would have us live as men who can just as well get along without Him. In a world come of age He helps us by His "weakness," that is, His willingness to be pushed out of the way (cf. *Letters and Papers from Prison*, Macmillan, 1967).

This is a remarkable position. Some judge it blasphemous. Others cannot square it with the scriptural revelation of a God who reveals Himself in Jesus Christ in order to seek and save mankind. Some hail it as a strategic theological mutation which will make it possible to remain a Christian in the totally secularized world of tomorrow. Whatever the response may be, Bonhoeffer is worthy of careful reading and intelligent appraisal.

How can people say that Christianity is better than other religions when they haven't looked into what others teach?

Very few Christians have more than a nodding acquaintance with other religious traditions. Buddhism and Hinduism, to say nothing of Taoism and Soka Gakki, are strange and exotic religions that belong on the other side of the globe.

One answer to the question posed is that having found reality in Christ there is little need to search elsewhere. Commitment to Christ involves a wholehearted acceptance of everything He taught: and did He not unequivocally declare, "No one comes to the Father, but by me"? (John 14:6).

This answer is not wrong. Christ *is* the truth and to know Him is to experience reality, which by definition rules out its opposite. The problem arises with the attitude in which this truth is held. Too often it fosters a sort of religious elitism which clogs the channels of effective communication with those who are without. I have always been intrigued by the testimony of the town clerk at Ephesus who, upon the occasion of the riot instigated by Demetrius the silver-smith, could say of Paul (after the apostle had preached in the city for three years) that he was neither sacrilegious or a blasphemer of their goddess, Artemis (Acts 19:37). While Paul could lash out at those who would pervert his gospel (cf. Gal. 5:12), he preferred not to alienate those he wanted to win by employing unnecessary polemics against their beliefs.

There is more than a modicum of truth in John Stuart Mill's remark, "He who knows only his side of the case, knows little of that" (from his essay, *On Liberty*). One of the values of at least some acquaintance with the major religious traditions of the world is the realization that the uniqueness of the Christian faith lies not in its ethical goal but in the action of God in history which supplies the power to achieve it.

The essential aspirations of most world religions are essentially the same. For example, the Bhagavad Gita of Hinduism counsels unconditional devotion as the way to final release:

> Worship better is than knowing,
> and renouncing better still.
> Near to renunciation—very near—
> dwelleth eternal Peace!

In Mahayana Buddhism the bodhisatt-vas—those having achieved sufficient merit to be eligible for Nirvana—turn back out of compassionate love, to serve the needs of suffering humanity.

These themes of trust and love are integral to Christianity as well. The point of difference lies in variant explanations of the human predicament which in turn determine a method of salvation. While Eastern religions see sin as rising out of ignorance, the Judeo-Christian tradition holds it to be a moral offense. Hence forgiveness, not education, is the answer. Forgiveness in a moral universe demands punishment for sin. The Christian answer involves nothing less than the Incarnation—that great event in which God entered His own creation in the person of Jesus Christ, took the punishment for man's sin and gave His life as a ransom. Resurrection is that shout of victory that sin and death have been defeated and that power to trust and love are now available for man.

The quality of life demanded by Christianity cannot be realized apart from supernatural enablement. Only the Christian answer is sufficiently radical to answer realistically man's tragic alienation from God, from his fellow man, and from his true self.

Some people claim that religious belief is a stage through which man is passing in his evolution from a primitive being to some highly sophisticated form not yet fully known. What do you think of this idea?

Man is essentially a religious being. History indicates that man needs to give his supreme allegiance to some power or being beyond himself. Atheism doesn't come naturally—it is an interpretation of reality which requires considerable rationalization.

On the other hand, it appears that modern man is less "religious" than his predecessors. At least he is far more willing to break with the accepted forms of religious practice. For a great many in the Western world, the church is a cultural anachronism carried over from a previous era by man's reluctance to let go of that which had meaning for a former generation.

Some definition is in order. By religion we may understand that sense of awe when confronted with a power or being of transcendent magnitude. It is the existential realization of human limitations in a world that reveals the presence and power of the supernatural. If this definition is adequate, then men are nonreligious only 1) when they have convinced themselves that nothing beyond the natural exists, or 2) when it is finally determined that we do in fact live in a universe which no longer requires the hypothesis of God as creator and sustainer.

An example of the first attitude is Stephen Crane's "Blustering God."

Blustering
god,
Stamping across the
sky

With loud
swagger,
I fear you
not.
No, though from your highest
heaven
You plunge your spear at my
heart,
I fear you
not.
No, not if the
blow
Is as the lightning blasting a
tree,
I fear you not, puffing
braggart.

As for the second possibility, I simply trust
myself to the self-revelation of God through
nature in a general way, through the incarnation in a specific historical way, and
through the continuing pressure of the Holy
Spirit via Scripture and personal encounter.
The forms of religious expression may alter
drastically in the next few years but man,
made in the image of God, will always be a
religious being. His need for God in the
twenty-first century will be as keen as it was in
the beginning of human history.

Is there any good in religions other than Christianity?

Like the well-known query, "Have you stopped beating your wife?" this question cannot be answered with a simple yes or no.

Although brought up on the particularism of the Christian faith ("there is no other name under heaven given among men by which we must be saved," Acts 4:12), many believers wonder at times about those in other religions who seem to be sincere in their desire to please God. Certainly there is value in any movement which lifts the moral and ethical plane of society. Who would discount the courage of a Stoic or the courtesy of a Confucianist? In Philippians 4:8 Paul quotes a list of virtues which may well have come from the pen of a Greek moralist. In advising the believers to "think about these things," he recognizes in the broadest sense the positive value of *the good* regardless of the immediate source.

However, that which may alleviate the tensions of society and that which restores personal fellowship with God are by no means one and the same. It was Jesus Himself who taught that "no one comes to the Father, but by me" (John 14:6). If *the good* be defined as "restored fellowship with God," then according to the teachings of the New Testament it is found only within the Christian faith.

The religions of man climb upward toward God: the gospel is the good news that God has come down to man. The chasm which could never have been spanned by human merit has been bridged by the infinite grace of a loving Father. Ultimately only this path is good.

The question of the uniqueness of the Judeo-Christian tradition has often been raised. Does the fact that God spoke through the Hebrew prophets imply that He did not speak to other peoples? Could the writers of Scripture have borrowed any of their material from other sources?

I have heard that Moses borrowed much of his legal material from Babylonian law codes. Would you comment on this?

The original question undoubtedly refers to the code of Hammurabi, a lengthy legal document inscribed on an eight-foot high stone pillar discovered just after the turn of the century in Susa, the ancient capital of Elam in southwest Iran. It apparently dates from the middle of the eighteenth century B.C. and therefore predates the Mosaic legislation by several hundred years.

In the prologue and epilogue of the 282-paragraph code, Hammurabi, the sixth and greatest king of the first dynasty of Babylon, is ascribed such beneficent titles as "protector of the weak" and "defender of the oppressed." The code itself is intended to promote justice and equality under law. Although women are not considered the equals of men they are accorded a remarkably high status for that stage of historical development. The laws relate to civil and commercial as well as criminal concerns.

There is no question that numerous similarities exist between the Code of Hammurabi and the Mosaic laws. This is what one would expect since all lists of ancient crimes along with the appropriate punishments would tend to resemble one another. It is the universal similarity of a limited variety of crimes and punishments that has at times led to the unwarranted conclusion that one has borrowed from the other. When the Mosaic legislation is compared with other ancient law codes of the Near East (not only that of Hammurabi, but also those of Ur-Nammu, Bilalama, and Lipit-Ishtar—all earlier than Hammurabi by several hundred years), it is found that Hebrew law was invariably more humane in spirit than its predecessors. In Exodus 20 at the opening of the Convenant Code we read that the Lord said to Moses, "Thus you shall say to the people of Israel" (Exod. 20:22). Thus the source for the three chapters of laws which follow is the mind and will of God, not some foreign code of jurisprudence.

I have heard that Mohammedans believe in Jesus. Is this true?

Islam is the world's second largest religion. It is strictly monotheistic and its adherents are characterized by absolute submission to the will of Allah. Mohammed was the last in a line of prophets which includes Jesus.

Islam teaches that down through time God has revealed His will through apostles who brought a written message. Jesus was one of these apostles. The Koran containing Mohammed's utterances is the completion of all that had gone before. It holds that both Jews and Christians have departed from the revelations they were given and must be brought back to the original truth as taught by Abraham. There is good evidence that Mohammed as a young man was deeply influenced by a monotheist, but Arabic tradition represents him as a man dissatisfied with both Judaism and Christianity.

Islam believes that Jesus Christ was an apostle sent by God. He was created not by any human generation but by the immediate action of God through His breath (the "holy spirit"). He was not crucified ("one was made to resemble him") nor did He ascend into heaven. Although the evidence is less than clear it seems that Jesus will appear on earth again prior to the day of judgment. In that the Koran teaches the absolute oneness of God, any belief in the redemptive work of

Christ (in the fully Christian sense) would be ruled out.

How can people who have been Christians leave the church and get mixed up in false religions?

While it is easy to understand how people brought up in another culture will regularly adopt the religious beliefs of that culture, it is harder to understand how believing Christians can fall away and join some questionable sect. While there is no single answer to the question posed (every case is different), a few general observations may be helpful.

Sometimes a person with a great longing for God fails to find within the church fellowship others who feel deeply about spiritual concerns. This may lead to a separation from the local church and a growing openness to fringe groups where religious commitment appears to be taken with more seriousness.

At other times we see the reverse. An individual not willing to accept a way of life understood and practiced by the local church will withdraw to a less-demanding group where he may have the advantage of feeling religious without adopting a pattern of conduct which he views as oppressive.

The important point is that these kinds of religious shifts are motivated not by doctrinal issues but by other considerations. There are some interesting passages in the Pastoral

Epistles which throw light on the discussion. In I Timothy 4 we learn that the subversive doctrines which were upsetting the church were inspired by demons (v. 1) but propagated by men of corrupt *conscience* (v. 2). It was by spurning *conscience* that certain people had made shipwreck of their faith (I Tim. 1:19). It was after turning from the truth that they wandered into myths (II Tim. 4:4) and gave heed to the "commands of men who reject the truth" (Titus 1:14).

Apparently doctrinal deviation is the result of ethical failure rather than intellectual impasse. The heretics in question were not men forced by the evidence to shift their theological position but men who had turned away from a clear understanding of what God wanted them to do.

This insight of Paul, that heresy stems from the volitional and emotional aspects of man rather than from the rational, is in harmony with much of the current thought in the field. Dagobert Runes, widely known philosopher from the University of Vienna, writes persuasively that since the thinking processes of man are universal, differences must result from the respective emotional grounds in which that thinking is rooted (*The Art of Thinking*, Citadel Press, n.d.). When a Christian leaves the faith, I would think that more often than not there is an all-important yet undisclosed ethical factor in his decision.

Isn't the demon possession of biblical times what we now call insanity or an uncontrollable temper?

Some years back, liberalism was quite satisfied that the idea of demon possession had been shelved along with other folk ideas such as planting by the light of the moon and throwing salt over the shoulder for good luck. But now the mood has changed. The spectacle of attempted racial genocide in Europe's most advanced and cultured country, the meteoric rise of astrology, and modern man's neurotic fascination with the occult, all indicate that he has by no means separated himself from the supranatural realm of malignant beings.

First we must understand what Scripture actually *says* about demons. Too often the past is caricatured by viewing it in terms of the present. Since "Red Hots" and "Orange Julius" picture the devil with tail, horns, and a red union suit, the unthinking demand that the people of the Bible conform to their cultural distortion of the past.

Contrary to the conventional wisdom that the further one presses back into history the more he will encounter such superstitions as "demon possession," nowhere in the Old Testament (except perhaps the "evil spirit from the Lord" which tormented Saul, I Sam. 16:14-15, and the "lying spirit in the mouth" of Ahab's prophets, I Kings 22:22ff.) is demon possession mentioned. Furthermore, apart from the Gospels, it is found only twice in the New Testament (Acts 16:16ff.; 19:13ff.).

Yet between these eras—that is, during the period of Christ's public ministry as recorded in the Gospels—we find extensive reference to demons and demon possession. In the four gospels demons are mentioned more than sixty times. Leon Morris correctly observes that demon possession "was a phenomenon especially associated with the earthly ministry of our Lord" and that it should be interpreted as "an outburst of demoniacal opposition to the work of Jesus" ("Devil" in *The New Bible Dictionary*, Eerdmans, 1962).

J. N. Geldenhuys, commenting on the man in the Capernaum synagogue "with an unclean spirit" which was cast out by Jesus (Luke 4:33-37), notes that since the Son of God came for the purpose of destroying the works of the devil (I John 3:8), the kingdom of the evil one would do everything possible to defeat Christ's plans. "Demon possession" says Geldenhuys "was one of the means used by the kingdom of darkness in this struggle" and Jesus, as Redeemer, had to cast out demons "to prove that He had indeed overcome the power of the evil one" (*Commentary on the Gospel of Luke*, Eerdmans, 1951).

To return to the original question: What about "demons" today? In that the Gospels clearly differentiate between organic maladies (such as disease, infection, epilepsy, and paralysis) and demonic possession (Matt. 4:24), it would be most unjustified to assume that what they held to be demonic we now call disease.

While demon possession might well in a given case produce something akin to insanity, to equate first-century possession and twentieth-century mental illness would be logically indefensible. It is instructive to note that it is Luke *the physician* who records more incidents of exorcism than any of the other Gospel writers.

Since the biblical evidence indicates that demon possession was a phenomenon connected with the earthly ministry of Christ, we may reasonably infer that it is not necessarily to be expected as a continuing experience in the history of the church. This is not, however, to rule out isolated instances, especially on mission fields where the gospel is waging offensive warfare against the darkness power of paganism.

Do you believe that there are people today who are actually possessed by demons?

For the person who approaches Scripture as a reliable source of information, there is little doubt that demons actually exist. Throughout the New Testament they appear as spiritual beings which are hostile to both

God and man. They are repeatedly said to *possess* certain people (Matt. 8:16; Mark 1:32), and on numerous occasions were cast out by Jesus (Mark 16:9; Luke 8:26-33; etc.).

Of the more than sixty references to demons in the New Testament, only ten are outside the four Gospels. There are few references to demon possession in the Old Testament. This suggests that at that very point in time when God was establishing His sovereignty over the forces of evil through the death and resurrection of His Son, history witnessed an unusual outburst of satanic opposition in the form of demon possession.

It is against this background that we should approach an answer to your question. First of all, what does Scripture say? In I Timothy 4:1 the apostle Paul states, "Now the Spirit expressly says that in later times some will depart from the faith by giving heed to deceitful spirits and doctrines of demons." The very next verse indicates that this demonically-inspired apostasy is carried out through the hypocrisy of lying teachers "whose consciences are as dead as seared flesh" (Phillips). While this does not speak of demon *possession*, it certainly emphasizes the activity of demons in the last days.

Revelation 12 tells of a war in heaven in which Satan is cast down to earth and a loud voice proclaims, "Woe to you, O earth and sea, for the devil has come down to you in great wrath, because he knows that his time is short!" (Rev. 12:12). The close of history will witness an awesome increase in satanic power and activity as the evil one concentrates his remaining energies in one final assault. As Christ at His first advent was met by widespread demon possession, it seems reasonable to assume that He will encounter a similar phenomenon when He returns a second time.

We may now ask if there are any indications today of a step-up in demonic activity. The extent to which occultism is being revived in our day is documented in the *Time* cover story of June 19, 1972. Voodoo dolls, astrology, best-seller novels such as *The Exorcist* (among the top ten for over a year) and *Rosemary's Baby*, psychic tours to Great Britain complete with a personal astro-numerology chart and seance, and Anton La Vey's First Church of Satan in San Francisco, all indicate a tremendous surge of interest in that which lies beyond the range of scientific scrutiny.

But is that demon possession? No, but what should we say about the twenty-two-year-old Miami woman Satanist who with self-confessed enjoyment killed a sixty-two-year-old friend by stabbing him forty-six times? Or, what of twenty-year-old Mike Newell who, after a brief service to the devil, had his friends bind him hand and foot and throw him into a New Jersey lake convinced that any loyal worshiper of Satan murdered by his friends would be reborn as a captain of devils? (*Newsweek*, July 19, 1971).

Psychological explanations there may be, but many competent observers of such grisly events are convinced that the mid-twentieth century is being revisited by those powers of evil which have always opposed the good but now are coming out into the open for a final showdown against the One who two thousand years ago emerged victorious from the crucial battle which ended not on Good Friday on the cross, but on Easter morning beside an empty grave.

6
Sin and Salvation

Central to any discussion of the human predicament, its origin and possible amelioration is the dual consideration of sin and salvation. That something has gone wrong is perfectly obvious. Pride, aggression, and deceit go all the way back to the first family. Why man acts as he does and what can be done about it fills the literature of religious movements.

Is sin the result of ignorance or is it the expression of willful self-centeredness? Is deliverance from sin the result of human striving or is it made possible by a supernatural act of God?

The questions which follow by no means exhaust the subject. They are not intended as a comprehensive overview of the biblical and theological perspective on soteriology. They do, however, represent valid and important concerns about man's basic problem (sin) and God's answer (salvation).

Is one sin as bad as another?

In a very real sense all sin is sin. Were a man to live a perfect life except for one minor flaw, he would still be barred from eternal fellowship with God. God's perfect holiness requires moral perfection. This no man can achieve. The Christian's approach to God is based upon the perfection of Jesus Christ appropriated through faith. Thus any sin, "large" or "small," separates a man from God.

That is not to say, however, that all sins are equally degrading or have the same social consequences. Raping an innocent child and dropping an idle remark can hardly be bracketed together in the same category. Both are wrong, but one is infinitely more serious in its personal and social ramifications.

People who announce that one sin is as bad as another are usually trying to put across the point that our judgments about certain sins may not be the same as God's (e.g., smoking versus excessive coffee drinking), or that we ought not to assume that "little" sins (venial?) are permissible while "big" sins (mortal?) are the only really dangerous ones.

The Bible states that a person is guilty of committing a sin if he thinks or wishes he could do a certain thing. Would you say that if you desire to perform a wrong act, you might as well go through with it, since you are already guilty?

In the Sermon on the Mount, Jesus taught that the negative restrictions of Jewish law were not enough to insure entrance into the kingdom of heaven (Matt. 5:20). Five times in one chapter we hear, "You have heard. . . . But I say to you" (Matt. 5:21-22, 27-28, 33-34, 38-39, 43-44).

In each case Jesus goes behind the legal prescription and deals with the underlying attitude. It is not enough to refrain from killing: kingdom righteousness demands the absence of anger, that malicious attitude from which the overt act arises. It is not enough *not* to commit adultery: man must be pure within, not given to looking at a woman with lust. In this "new morality" Jesus strikes at the very citadel of sin—the inner reaches of one's soul.

It does not follow, however, that the momentary desire to sin is, in God's sight, the equivalent of the act itself. A propensity towards evil is part of our fallen human nature. Temptations arise but are not in themselves sin. They become sin when we begin to toy with the possibility. The longer we hesitate in rejecting the possibility, secretly and vicariously indulging ourselves by way of anticipation, the greater our sin becomes.

While the act itself is the end result of growing desire, it is usually only the final decision to throw caution to the wind and willfully disobey what we know to be right. Hence the initial temptation becomes sin when consciously entertained, compounded as we dwell on the possibility, and reaches fulfillment when we defy all restraint.

To view all sin as equally bad may serve to remind us that even "little sins" are offensive in the sight of God, but it also tends to blur some important distinctives. The suggestion that once a sin is desired we might as well have the fun of going through with it fails to understand the nature of sin and, if seriously contemplated, displays an appalling lack of moral sensitivity.

What are the seven deadly sins?

The seven deadly sins are listed as pride, covetousness, lust, envy, gluttony, anger, and sloth.

Early in the life of the church the influence of Greek thought, with its tendency to view sin as a necessary flaw in human nature, made it necessary for the church to determine the relative seriousness of various moral faults. This ultimately gave rise to the seven deadly sins.

The designation "deadly" should not be understood in the Roman Catholic sense of "mortal." Rather, the sins are deadly in the sense that they are the primary sinful drives which are most likely to give rise to particular sinful acts.

What would you say about a person who has trouble feeling sorry for his sins?

Feeling sorry is an emotional reaction which in and of itself has no particular merit. Only as it reflects a deeper reorientation of values does it take on any special significance. The world is full of people who feel sorry about things they have done. Sometimes it is genuine, but quite often there are other reasons for wishing to undo the past. Some people are sorry only because they have gotten trapped by the wrong they did. It is not the wrongness of the act but the shame of its consequences which bothers. Still others use sorrow and remorse as a sort of self-flagellation to atone for wrongdoing. This kind of neurotic sorrow has no virtue.

Since religious experience involves the whole man, and emotions are a real part of the total experience, it is quite easy to be misled into thinking that emotion is central to religion. This is not so. The biblical idea of repentance is a right about-face. It is primarily a reorientation of the will, not an alleviation of the pangs of conscience. Repentance for sin will undoubtedly affect the emotions but is in no sense to be equated with that particular response.

There may be several reasons why a person has trouble feeling sorry for his sins. It may be that he doesn't realize that sin is a personal offense against God, not the breaking of some impersonal law. A Christian cannot sin without betraying his closest Friend and slamming the door on life's most meaningful relationship. The answer is to enter more fully into a personal understanding of the biblical teaching about God and sin.

Or it may be that the person is one of those rare and honest individuals who won't join the lock step parade of ecclesiastical conformity. The important thing is not that he should feel a certain way about a breach in Christian conduct, but that he wills not to sin.

It is the dawning realization of the greatness of God's love, supremely manifested in allowing His Son to become sin, that draws us away from sin and teaches us to hate every unworthy deed, word, or thought. As we increasingly understand the dimensions of divine love, we will increasingly despise every failure to live as sons of God. However, even here the measure of our love is indicated by the set of our will and not the emotional response which may follow.

What exactly is the new birth? What happens within a man when he is born again?

The term "new birth" is a metaphor which describes the redemptive re-creation of a man's fallen human nature and his consequent restoration to fellowship with God. It is that decisive event which takes place in a man's inner being (Rom. 12:2) when, by the divine action of the Holy Spirit (Titus 3:5), he is constituted a new creation in Christ Jesus (II Cor. 5:17) in true righteousness and holiness after the likeness of God (Eph. 4:24).

The clearest illustration of what the new birth involves is seen in the encounter between Jesus and Nicodemus (John 3). Here we learn that however laudatory religious learning and sincerity may be, they do not in themselves constitute the new birth (John 3:3). An important clue is to be found in the Greek word translated "anew" (John 3:3, 7; *anōthen*). It bears the double meaning of "again" (in point of time) and "from above" (in respect to its divine source and essential nature). From this we infer two things. First, that the new birth is a quality of existence which we do not possess as a result of our first, or natural, birth. By nature man is "dead in trespasses and sins" (Eph. 2:1). Second, that it is a birth into a higher sphere— the sphere of the Spirit. By natural birth we became members of the human race with all its aspirations for nobility yet with its propensity toward self-deification. Regardless of the magnitude or our ethical achievement within this sphere, we still fall short of the standard for divine acceptance. But by the "new birth" we enter a completely different realm of existence. It is life in the Spirit! We are said to be "in Christ," that is, vitally related to God Himself by virtue of the indwelling Holy Spirit.

No metaphor less vivid than birth could adequately express the amazing transformation of a man upon whom the Spirit of God has moved with life-giving power.

No metaphor less vivid than birth could adequately express the amazing transformation of a man upon whom the Spirit of God has moved with life-giving power.

How were people saved in the Old Testament?

In Hebrews 11 it is said of Enoch that "before he was taken he was attested as having pleased God. And without faith it is impossible to please him" (11:5b-6a). Faith is the response that God requires of all men. In Genesis 15 we have the account of God taking Abram outside under the starry canopy of the evening sky: "Do you see all those stars, Abram? That's how many descendants you'll have!" This was a staggering promise to an old man whose wife was past the age of bearing children. Yet Scripture records that "he believed the Lord; and he reckoned it to him as righteousness" (v. 6). This great act of faith becomes pivotal in Paul's development of justification by faith alone (cf. Rom. 4:3; Gal. 3:6).

What did Abram believe? He believed exactly what God had told him—that his descendants would be as numerous as the stars of heaven. This absurd confidence in what was humanly impossible is what made him righteous in God's sight. Faith is taking God at His word. Thus it appears to me that people in the Old Testament were saved by simple faith in whatever God asked of them. While all men of every era are saved on the basis of Christ's atoning death, the exact content of their faith is determined by the stage of progressive revelation in which they find themselves.

The sacrificial system instituted through Moses did not in itself bring salvation (Heb. 10:4). It provided an opportunity for the response of obedience while at the same time pointed beyond itself to the one great sacrifice which alone would atone for the sins of man. Throughout the Old Testament (as it is today) it was faith alone that made a man acceptable in God's sight.

If grace is unmerited favor, how can it obligate a person to change his life?

This is precisely the question that was put to Paul by his opponents. They were convinced that a man found favor in the sight of God by measuring up to certain prescribed standards. Paul insisted in Romans 6 that righteousness was a free gift of God received by faith alone.

So they pressed what they felt were the implications of his position: "Are we to continue in sin that grace may abound?" (v. 1b). If God's grace is magnified by being greater than all our sin, then let's get busy sinning to demonstrate that grace is inexhaustible. Paul answers, "By no means! How can we who died to sin still live in it?" (v. 2).

The very suggestion arises from a faulty understanding of grace. Grace is not a commodity—like a new hat—but a transforming power. To experience the dynamic of grace is to undergo a total reorientation of life.

Grace obligates in the same way that love obligates. The wellspring of obligation is within the changed person. He *wants* to respond nobly to his encounter with divine grace. He can't help it: grace itself has made him a new man. That the compulsion to live worthily of the unmerited favor he has received rises from within rather than from demands pressed on from without does not alter the fact that the dynamic of grace creates an atmosphere of obligation. Bonhoeffer has reminded us that "cheap grace" is no part of the gospel of our Lord Jesus Christ.

I know it's an old chestnut, but can a person lose his salvation?

Augustine, bishop of Hippo in northern Africa and a towering figure in early Christian thought (354-430), held that God bestowed on those whom he had elected to salvation the gift of final perserverance. That is, believers could rest in the confidence that God would never allow them to fall away. Augustine's logic has convinced a major portion of Christendom, but not all. Some believe that man's free will allows him to step out of a saving relationship with God as it also allowed him to step in. Augustine's major protagonist was Pelagius, a British lay monk, who taught that it was man who took the initial step towards God, unaided by divine grace. If man took the first step toward God, he could also take the first step away. So the question continues: can a person lose his salvation?

A. M. Hunter writes of the three tenses of salvation—past, present, and future (*Interpreting Paul's Gospel,* Westminister Press, 1955, pp.21-55). When Paul writes to Timothy of "God, who saved us" (II Tim. 1:8-9), the reference is to salvation as an event which took place in the *past*.

But there is also a salvation yet *future*. To the Romans Paul writes that "salvation is nearer to us now than when we first believed" (Rom. 13:11).

However, the noun *salvation* and its corresponding verb forms, are regularly used of a deliverance which takes place in the *present*. "For the word of the cross is folly to those who are perishing, but to us *who are being saved* [the Twentieth century New Testament reads "who are in the path of Salvation"] it is the power of God" (Cor. 1:18, italics mine). Here salvation is something happening *now*.

The usual translation of Ephesians 2:8, "For by grace you have been saved," fails to bring out the emphasis of the Greek periphrastic perfect (*este sesōsmenoi*) which according to J. H. Moulton in *Grammar of the New Testament Greek: Prolegomena* (T. and T. Clark, 1908-63, p. 127) refers to "a work which is finished on its Author's side, but progressively realized by its objects."

We may conclude without hesitancy that Scripture in its totality knows of no past salvation which will someday issue in a future salvation which does not pass through a continuing present tense salvation. A comprehensive understanding of the doctrine includes what has happened, what is happening and what will happen. A deliverance as all-embracing as this cannot be lost until it is fully realized. Since final salvation is yet future the question of losing it is for the present premature.

Does not Philippians 2:12 ("Work out your own salvation with fear and trembling") indicate that what we do has at least some bearing on our salvation?

I agree that man is not a passive agent in salvation. Salvation is always received by faith (Phil. 3:9), and this faith inevitably leads to a life of practical righteousness.

The verse quoted, however, does not deal with personal salvation. The context suggests that Paul has in mind the corporate deliverance of the church at Philippi from the initial stages of disunity. Unchecked, this disunity could lead to a serious schism in the church. The threat is seen in warnings to be of "one mind" (1:27; 2:2), Paul's plea to Euodia and Syntyche to "agree in the Lord" (4:2), and the inclusion of Christ's great example of self-renunciation (2:5-11) in order to buttress His exhortation to "count others better than yourselves" (2:3).

The word "salvation" in Philippians 2:12 has the wider meaning of "deliverance" as it does in 1:19 (cf. also Heb. 11:7 where the same Greek word occurs).

Thus Paul is saying, "Following the example of Christ who exchanged the glories of heaven for death on a cross, count the other fellow worthy of preferential treatment and keep on working out (*katergadzesthe*, present tense) your own deliverance from the state of disunity which threatens the life of the church. Do it with fear and trembling because it is God Himself who is at work in your midst."

Is forgiveness absolutely free or is there something which man must do to be forgiven?

That there is nothing that man can do to *merit* forgiveness is the clear teaching of Scripture. In Ephesians 2:5 Paul writes, "Even when we were dead through our trespasses God made us alive together with Christ" and the Colossian parallel adds "having forgiven us all our trespasses" (Col. 2:13).

The aorist participle (*charisamenos*) in this context indicates that both our regeneration and forgiveness as events in God's time were effected when Christ went to the cross. If it were necessary for us to do something to make forgiveness possible, then His work of redemption would be faulty.

Notice, however, that while forgiveness as a divine act is an accomplished fact, it is by no means automatically applied to all. It must be received. And what receiving entails is also clearly taught in Scripture. To those who heard Peter's sermon on the day of Pentecost and, cut to the heart, cried out, "What shall we do?" Peter answered, *"Repent.* . . . for the forgiveness of your sins" (Acts 2:38, italics mine). On a subsequent occasion he warned his listeners, *"Repent therefore,* and turn again, that your sins may be blotted out" (Acts 3:19, italics mine). To Simon the magician who tried to buy the gift of the Holy Spirit, Peter admonished, *"Repent . . . that, if possible, the intent of your heart may be forgiven you"* (Acts 8:22, italics mine.).

Forgiveness of sin is everywhere tied to genuine repentance. Not that repentance is a "work" which merits forgiveness—it is rather that attitude of serious regret for our waywardness that allows us to accept what God has already accomplished. While it would be psychologically unwise to encourage neurotic guilt, it would be equally unwise to remove repentance as a prerequisite for forgiveness.

I received several letters regarding the answer immediately above in which I maintained that repentance was a necessary prerequisite for forgiveness. The objections had nothing to do with the basic point I was attempting to establish, but rather with my use of Scripture.

One letter said, "In quoting from Acts 2:38 you said, 'Repent . . . for the forgiveness of your sins.' This is most unfortunate in as much as Peter said, 'Repent, and be baptized . . . for the forgiveness of your sins.' The apostle tied these two actions together as prerequisites for forgiveness." At the end of the letter the reader said, "I believe that those who would teach others owe it to their students to tell them what the Lord has said, and all that the Lord has said."

Two things should be said to help explain what I believe to be a misunderstanding.

1. It was not my intention to alter Scripture by omission. In the verses quoted I specifically indicated the deletions by the customary practice of substituting three dots.

2. The purpose for omitting the phrase on baptism was to throw into bold relief the relationship between repentance and forgiveness. A discussion of baptism was not germane to the question. It was not my purpose to develop a theological statement on all that is involved in salvation: I merely wanted to show from Scripture that forgiveness apart from repentance is an unreal fantasy. By deleting those parts of the verses which did not speak to the point in question, I hoped to establish in clear form the relevant scriptural teaching.

In fact, in the context of the question posed, the forgiveness of which I wrote was not necessarily limited to the salvation experience but referred more broadly to the kind of general forgiveness intended by a verse like I John 1:9.

Now I will speak to the theological point implicit in the responses of those who objected to my omissions. The issue may be posed in the form of the question: "Is baptism necessary for salvation?"

That baptism is a necessary and integral part of the requirements for salvation seems to be the thrust of such verses as Acts 2:38;

22:16; Gal. 3:27; etc. A segment of the Christian Church has taken these verses rather literally to mean that apart from the rite of baptism there is no salvation. A major objection to this interpretation is that it represents an unconscious lapse into legalism. The major difference between the old and new covenant is the movement from the external and legalistic to the inner and spiritual. To require a ritual act as a *sine qua non* of salvation represents the lingering influence of the "dispensation of condemnation" (II Cor. 3:9).

Most of Protestant Christianity interprets baptism in a symbolic fashion. It becomes an outward testimony to an inner transformation. It symbolizes death to the old life beneath the malignant control of sin and resurrection to the new life made possible by the indwelling Spirit of God. Salvation does not depend on the rite; the rite gives symbolic expression to salvation.

Can you cite several verses from the New Testament which show that good works are a necessary part of the Christian life?

One unfortuate result of an over-emphasis on what is popularly called "once saved, always saved," is the tendency of some to deny the importance of a transformed life. One young person I knew decided he could strike a bargain with God and announced that he had chosen to "have a good time on earth and take a back seat in heaven!"

The relationship between faith and works has been debated since the dawn of free discussion. The irresistible force of Paul's "man is not justified by works of the law but through faith in Jesus Christ" (Gal. 2:16) meets the immovable object of James' "man is justified by works and not by faith alone" (James 2:24). The tension is resolved when we accept the fact that while man is saved by faith alone, no man is saved by a faith which is alone.

Faith-works is a hyphenated concept in which the latter element grows out of and gives expression to the former. There is among evangelicals in our day, however, a tendency to be so absorbed in the doctrine of faith that we neglect the equally important teaching about works. The same Paul who desired to be found in Christ with a righteousness not based on law but depending on faith (Phil. 3:9) also insisted that believers are created in Christ Jesus for the express purpose of good works (Eph. 2:10). As the people of God we are to be "zealous for good deeds" (Tit. 2:14). In fact, Romans 2:6ff. tells us that final judgment will be on the basis of works (*kata ta erga*). No man will ever be accepted into the presence of God on the basis of what he has done; nevertheless, the quality of every man's faith will be determined by the way his faith expresses itself in works. Peter refers to God as the One who "judges each one impartially according to his deeds" (I Pet. 1:17).

Perhaps the strongest emphasis on a faith that acts comes from the lips of Jesus Himself. He concludes the Sermon on the Mount with three basic thrusts: 1) The quality of a man's life is known by the fruit which it produces (Matt. 7:15-20). 2) Only those who do the will of God—not those who merely claim great exploits—will enter the kingdom of heaven (Matt. 7:21-23). 3) The difference between the house that stands and the house that falls is the difference between hearing and *doing* and hearing only (Matt. 7:24-27).

In Jesus' parable of the sower (Matt. 13) the seed sown on the rocky ground and on the thorny ground did not produce fruit. Can there be genuine growth which does not ultimately lead to salvation?

The parable as told (vv. 3-9) and interpreted (vv. 18-23) by Jesus does not have as its purpose information about who is going to be saved. The exhortation of verse 9 ("He who has ears, let him hear") and the fact that Jesus was speaking to a large crowd composed of people who had gathered for various reasons (v. 2) indicates that the parable teaches four ways to hear the Word of God. It is as relevant to the Christian as to the non-Christian.

Is it not true that more often than we would like to admit the Word of God proclaimed in a Sunday morning service is snatched away by the birds of inattention and postworship tom-foolery? And how often is our commitment too quickly given to be able to withstand an ensuing period of tribulation? What about the cares of the world and the delight in riches? The parable teaches us all to prepare carefully the ground of our soul that the divine Seed will take root, grow, and yield fruit.

What do you think of the idea that although the conscious mind is given to God at conversion, a subsequent act is necessary to convert the subconscious mind?

Paul defines the sons of God as "all who are *led* (that is, "are being led," Greek, *agontai*, present tense) by the Spirit of God" (Rom. 8:14).

Whether this growth at some point *requires* a specific crisis doesn't seem to be taught in Scripture, although interestingly enough it appears to have been the experience of a great number of people (not all Wesleyan by any means). I would guess that sanctification rarely progresses at a steady pace. Most believers in retrospect can recall the periods of significant spiritual advance. However, to say that such a crisis represents the conversion of the subconscious mind strikes me as psychologically (if not biblically) unwarranted. My suspicion is that the old man never gives up. He may be "rendered inoperative" (Rom. 6:6, *katargeō*) but he has unusual recuperative powers. E. Stanley Jones is right in saying that "the problem of victorious living centers, then, in one thing chiefly: self-surrender," but self-surrender is a continuing acknowledgment of the lordship of Christ rather than a single act which converts the subconscious mind.

What exactly is the "limited atonement," and is it biblical?

The doctrine of the limited atonement teaches that Christ died for the purpose of saving only those elected to salvation. Along with total depravity, unconditional election, irresistible grace, and the perserverance of the saints, it is part of the basic theological structure of Calvinism. David Steele and Curtis Thomas state the doctrine this way: "Historical or main line Calvinism has consistently maintained that Christ's redeeming work was definite in *design* and *accomplishment*—that it was intended to render complete satisfaction for certain specified sinners and that it actually secured salvation for these individuals and for no one else" (*The Five Points of Calvinism: Defined, Defended, Documented*, Presbyterian and Reformed, 1963,

p. 39). It is generally supported by such arguments as 1) the designs of God cannot be frustrated by the actions of man; 2) Scripture continually qualifies those for whom Christ died, e.g., "the sheep" in John 10:11, "the church" in Acts 20:28, and; 3) if Christ died for all then it follows logically that all men are actually saved (cf. Louis Berkhof, *Systematic Theology*, Eerdmans, 1941, pp.394-95).

While the Reformed wing of the Church has been willing to accept the doctrine of a limited atonement, the majority of contemporary Christians have not. Verses such as I John 2:2, "He [Jesus Christ the righteous] is the propitiation for our sins: and not for ours only, but also for the sins of the whole world," (KJV) and II Corinthians 5:19, "God was in Christ reconciling the world unto himself," (KJV) are too difficult to explain away. Further, the idea of offering salvation through the proclamation of the gospel to those who couldn't receive it anyway (even though Scripture clearly says "whosoever shall call upon the name of the Lord shall be saved," Acts 2:21, KJV) is a sort of divine charade that places the character of God in question. The desire for rational control of God and His activity has more than once forced a "reinterpretation" of the obvious meaning of Scripture.

Can children gradually become Christians, or do they have to have a specific conversion experience?

Before answering your specific question, I would like to use it as an example of one of the major semantic problems in biblical interpretation. Consider the word "conversion." In other contexts it would mean "the reduction of a mathematical expression by the cleansing of fractions," or "scoring on the try for an extra point after touchdown." In the context of religious discourse, however, it refers to that experience associated with the definite and decisive adoption of religion. We speak of a person being converted to the Christian faith. His conversion involves a clean break from his former way of life and whole-hearted acceptance of Jesus as Lord.

Some conversions are dramatic. Paul was struck blind by a light from heaven while on the road to Damascus (Acts 9:1-9). Certain evangelists were won over from a life of gross sin and find it effective to stress the dramatic difference between life then and now. Against this background it is no wonder, that upon reading such verses as Matthew 18:3 ("Except ye be converted . . . ye shall not enter into the kingdom of heaven," KJV), or Acts 3:19 ("Repent . . . and be converted, that your sins may be blotted out," KJV), people are inclined to believe that a "conversion experience" (in some such form as outlined above) is necessary for salvation.

But does Scripture support this point of view, especially as it relates to children? When we examine the various forms of the word *conversion* in the New Testament, we learn that in the nine places where the King James Version uses convert/converted/converteth, other (and later) translations use expressions such as turn or return. The Greek word is *epistrephō* (only in Matt. 18:3 is the simpler *strephō* used), which means to turn about or return. In the New Testament both repentance and conversion speak of an essential change of direction: the first tends to denote the inward change, and the latter the wider and more inclusive redirection of one's total being. Conversion is not a synonym of salvation. In Acts 3:19 conversion leads to the forgiveness of sins. In Luke 22:32 Jesus prays that Peter's faith may not fail and that when he is "converted" (KJV)—when he has "turned again" (RSV)—he will strengthen his brethren. It seems clear, then, that we often unwittingly read into the phraseology of the older translation a meaning of conversion which, although proper in religious discourse, is not what Scripture is talking about.

A closely related problem is our tendency to confuse the psychological factors of religious conversion with the objective fact of accepting Christ. The extent of the psychological reorientation depends upon a number of factors, such as the emotional makeup of the person, the length of time that he has actively resisted the call of God, etc. A grown man, who for many years has lived in gross wickedness haunted by the memories of a praying mother, will—in coming to Christ —undoubtedly go through a soul-shattering experience. The psychological repercussions are great because of accumulated guilt and a conscience which has been abused and defiled for many years.

But what of children? Are we to expect them to weep over their sin, sense a terrible lostness, and then emerge on the other side of "conversion" as born-again believers? I think not! There need be no abrupt break as they gradually pass over from the enjoyment of an inherited love of Jesus to a personal faith in Christ as Lord. The pattern of adult conversion, especially in its dramatic form, should not be pressed upon children as the way to be saved. Let them grow to know and love the Lord as a natural response to a heavenly Father who loved them so much that He made it possible for them to spend eternity with Him in heaven.

Do babies go to heaven?

I imagine that almost every Christian from time to time ponders the destiny of babies or children who die at a very young age. Certainly, God would not exclude them from heaven. But what of the millions of babies born in non-Christian lands whose parents are members of other religions? If these children live, chances are they will worship as their parents do. But if they die, will they go to heaven the same as the infants of Christian parents?

The Scriptures are remarkably quiet about a lot of things which we would like to understand, but are not necessary for Christian growth and maturity. The fate of children who die at an early age is certainly one of these. It appears, however, that God is more concerned that we grow in the Christian graces than that we develop a comprehensive theology. Paul warns us against idle speculation and emphasizes, "The aim of our charge is love that issues from a pure heart" (I Tim. 1:5).

In checking through several standard textbooks in systematic theology I discovered that no one is anxious to commit himself to a serious argument on the subject of the status of children who die before they commit conscious sin. All seem more or less ready to agree that God would not consign to hell children who die before reaching some acceptable stage of accountability. The reluctance to discuss the issue undoubtedly stems from the lack of scriptural passages which speak directly to the issue.

Even in the related but less crucial question of infant baptism, as strong a Calvinist theologian as Berkhof admits that "there is no explicit command in the Bible to baptize children" and that "there is not a single instance in which we are plainly told that children were baptized" (*Systematic Theology*, Eerdmans, 1941). Yet he insists that this lack does not make infant baptism unbiblical. In the same way most theologians would insist that the lack of any specific scriptural foundation does not indicate that God must therefore be sitting idly by as children who have not had the opportunity to either hear or reject are herded into the fires of hell. That in itself would be doctrine unsupported by Scripture.

Why then do people believe that babies who die go to heaven? My own answer is that it is an inference based upon what we know of God as revealed in Scripture. I imagine that most believers would resist the idea of annihilation of deceased infants. Once life begins it continues even beyond the grave. Those who accept Christ enjoy eternal life and those who refuse to acknowledge God suffer eternal punishment (which involves conscious existence). Thus it seems that the baby who dies must also enter into one of these two states. If there is some third alternative we know nothing of it from Scripture. The specter of a newborn babe suffering eternal punishment is entirely unacceptable in a moral universe. We could never conceive of a God whose nature is love, planning or allowing such a hideous miscarriage of justice. Therefore we accept the alternative—that is, that babies are accepted into God's presence on the basis of Christ's atoning work even though they are incapable of exercising personal faith in Him.

Some have suggested that only those babies who if they lived would have accepted Christ are taken into heaven. This overly deterministic and rather mechanical point of view receives little support. Others have said that the high rate of infant mortality in primitive cultures and unevangelized tribes may be God's way of tricking the devil and winning for Himself followers from every tribe and nation. I would be inclined to label this as unsportsman-like conduct!

Two questions are closely related: What of those who are the victims of serious mental retardation, and, what of those who never hear the gospel? Does God also accept these without the requirement of personal faith?

I would assume that the mentally retarded would fall into the same class as the infants and would not be excluded from God's grace because of an option that was never theirs. The unbelieving "heathen," however, are a different lot. Paul explicitly tells us that they are without excuse. They have rejected God's self-revelation in nature and turned to religious substitutes, immoral relations, and all manner of evil (Rom. 1:19-32). (What happens to those who respond affirmatively to the limited revelation they receive is another matter, and deserves more thorough discussion.) The point is that those who do not hear the gospel are not to be placed in the same category with babies who are unable to act on any level of revelation.

Is the practice of baptizing children scriptural?

Those who advocate infant baptism present such evidence as 1) Paul's statement that the children were admitted to the covenant community; and 4) the lack of any suggestion in the New Testament that young people are to seek baptism at the age of accountability. the New Testament counterpart to Old Testament circumcision—the rite by which children were admitted to the convenant community; and 4) the lack of any suggestion in the New Testament that yourn people are to seek baptism at the age of accountability.

Baptists and other groups have rejected infant baptism because 1) the New Testament nowhere expressly commands the baptism of children nor does it offer a single clear cut example that it was ever practiced in the apostolic church; 2) as an outward expression of that inward change by which the believer enters the kingdom of God, it presupposes genuine repentance and faith; 3) the conjuction of "making disciples" and "baptizing them" in verses such as Matthew 28:19 is most naturally interpreted as belonging together in point of time; and 4) the baptism of infants encourages a superstitious confidence in the efficacy of the external rite.

Documents of the postapostolic church indicate that infant baptism was widely practiced in the second and third centuries. Origen, a famous Christian scholar who wrote voluminously during the first half of the third century, states that infant baptism was by then the established custom of the church (*Hom. in Lev.*, viii.4). Those opposing the practice are quick to point out that this phenomenon coincided with the rise of sacramentalism in the church and represents a departure from the truth rather than normative Christianity itself.

7
What About the Future?

Eschatology is the study of the last things. It has always held a special appeal for people. Our natural curiosity leads us to garner all the information we can about the close of this age and the dawn of the eternal state. Some of the popular spokesmen for specific views go beyond the evidence and come to regard their own conjectures as established fact. The result is considerable confusion on the part of the lay audience trying to gain insight into how history will come to a close.

The questions which follow treat some of the major themes of eschatology. Hopefully they will bring understanding, not add to the confusion.

Do you believe that the second coming of Christ is imminent?

It seems to me that the return of Christ has always been imminent. Throughout the New Testament the parousia is pictured as an event within the forseeable future. The last thing that Jesus says in the Book of Revelation is, "Surely I am coming soon" (Rev. 22:20).

Imminence, however, is not primarily a chronological concept. At 2:59 on an average summer afternoon it would be unsuitable to speak of three o'clock as being imminent. If tomorrow is just another today, it may arrive on schedule but it is not imminent. Only significant events are truly imminent, and the quality of imminence is related more to the nature of the event itself than to the particular day on which it happens.

In that the next great redemptive event following the resurrection will be the return of Christ, it is correct to say that this return is imminent. After two thousand years it may be closer in point of time, but it is not more imminent. In every period of history men have rightly looked forward to the consummation. The imminence of this great event has permeated the church with a sense of urgency in carrying out its mission.

Imminence is not dependent upon the calendar: it is the realization that the return of Christ is the great culminating event which brings meaning to human history and marks the entrance into a new sphere of existence.

How do you explain Jesus' statement in Luke 21:32 that "this generation will not pass away till all has taken place"?

In the immediate context Jesus has just described the fall of Jerusalem, cosmic disturbances of unprecedented proportions, men fainting with fear, and the coming of the Son of man in a cloud with power and great glory. This is followed with the parable of the fig tree, teaching that as the leaf heralds the coming of summer so believers may know by observation that the kingdom of God is near. In fact, "this generation will not pass away till all has taken place."

The difficulty is obvious: that generation *did pass away* without all the events taking place. Many solutions have been offered. One claims that the generation under question is the one which will be present when these things *begin* to take place some time in the future. That is, once the eschatological events begin, it will be no more than one generation until all is completed. Another solution understands "generation" in the sense of "race" and sees in the verse a promise that the Jewish people will be around until the very end. I am more satisfied with the suggestion of A. R. C. Leaney in *A Commentary on the Gospel According to Luke*

(Harper New Testament Commentary, Harper and Brothers, 1958) that Luke uses *genea* to mean "mankind." In other words, the kingdom of God will most certainly come within the history of mankind. It is a way of emphasizing the certainty of the kingdom. The promise is further strengthened in the following verse which adds, "Heaven and earth will pass away, but my words will not pass away."

Should the Lord's return bring us into line?

The majority of evangelists and speakers at prophetic conferences are thoroughly convinced that we have now entered the last phase of human history. Their congregations and constituencies are persuaded by the evidence as well. "What If It Were Today!" is sung with conviction and joyful expectancy.

The soon return of Jesus Christ has apparently been a firm conviction of the church from the very beginning. Two of Jesus' most enigmatic statements are not unrelated to this expectation. In sending out the Twelve on a preaching mission Jesus said they would not have gone through all the towns of Israel before the Son of man would come (Matt. 10:23). A bit later He told the same group that some of them would not taste death before they would see the Son of man coming in His kingdom (Matt. 16:28). In one of his first letters Paul spoke of "we who are alive, who are left until the coming of the Lord" (I Thess. 4:15)—a group in which he most certainly included himself! And in the last chapter of the New Testament is the promise, "Behold, I am coming soon" (Rev. 22:7).

Verses such as these—and there are many more—highlight the fact that from the beginning an expectation of the end of history has permeated the Christian church. Especially during those times when the church has taken Scripture with all seriousness this expectation has burned with an even greater intensity.

I am not suggesting that since the hopes of the early church were not fulfilled within its life span that we are to infer that the present expectations of the second coming are likewise doomed to disappointment. I *am* saying that inner assurance itself will not force God's hand. That much, at least, history has established. Christ may come soon—and I believe He will—but He need not because I think He will.

How should the possibility of an imminent return affect the way believers live? Ideally it should not make one whit of difference. Christian conduct is the net result of the transforming power of God's eternal Spirit in the human heart and the believer's willingness to surrender his stubborn will to God. Ideally God is in complete control. This is what the lordship of Jesus Christ is all about. The fact that Christ may return now or later has nothing to do with the believer's obligation to conform to the will and nature of God.

Unfortunately we find ourselves only sporadically and for limited periods approaching this ideal. So some would ask, Shouldn't the soon return of Christ serve as a motivating force to bring us into line?

Again I would have to register a serious reservation. This approach seems to say that what is really important is to be in good shape at that particular point in time when Christ returns. It's the old I-don't-want-to-be-caught-in-there-when-Jesus-returns syndrome. It suggests in a veiled way that the mark we get on our ethical report card is the mark we happen to receive on the pop quiz given at the parousia rather than the cumulative grade for the entire course.

This may be a poor analogy but the intent is to say that our lives are open and fully known to God and that His concern is for our lifelong growth and spiritual maturity. By nature we were rebels. Rebellion can be quelled only by a fundamental change of attitude. This change begins at conversion and continues throughout the entire life. What is of supreme importance is our willingness to present ourselves daily to the One whose deepest desire is to help us conform to the

image of His Son (Rom. 8:28)—and that for
our good.

Peter talked of the day of the Lord when
the heavens would pass away with a loud
noise and the earth would be dissolved with
fire (II Peter 3:10). This being the case he
poses the rhetorical question, "What sort of
persons ought you to be in lives of holiness
and godliness!" (v. 11). Note, however, that it
is the fact of the day of the Lord and all it entails, rather than the imminence, which un-
dergirds the ethic. Believers are to "grow in
the grace and knowledge of our Lord and
Savior Jesus Christ" not in order to be in
good ethical shape on the day He returns,
but because of the inexorable logic which
flows from the transitory nature of the
present creation and the eternal nature of
the spiritual. We are to live godly lives
because no other lifestyle is appropriate, not
in order to make it in under the wire.

Will the temple in Jerusalem be rebuilt?

The answer given to this question depends
on one's larger approach to the interpretation of prophecy. For some, prophecy is
prewritten history. The claim is that the
morning newspaper can be read side by side
with biblical prophecy and cross-referenced
in a dozen places every day.

Others see the fulfillment of prophecy in
larger trends and the development of

ideologies. In this case the content of prophecy is distinguished from its cultural expression. Telstar and the jet airplane are not to be sought in the unexplored depths of prophetic speech.

The former approach envisions the rebuilding of the temple and the reinstitution of ancient Jewish ritual in the future. The latter is content to explain passages such as Ezekiel 40–48 as fulfilled in Zerubbabel's temple, the church, or eternity itself.

If all the saved go to heaven and the unrighteous go to hell, why is there to be a new earth? (II Peter 3:13; Rev. 21:1; Isa. 65:17; 66:22).

The concept of new heavens and a new earth stems from Isaiah 65 and 66. Over against the unfaithfulness of Israel and its inevitable result of sorrow and desolation (cf. Isa. 64:10), the prophet foretells the day when God will create all things anew. Heaven and earth will be transformed, God will rejoice (Isa. 65:19; cf. 62:5), and man will live securely in a paradisiacal environment (Isa. 65:20-25).

This concept of a new creation is found with some regularity in extrabiblical literature as well. For example, "The first heaven will depart and pass away, and a new heaven will appear, and all the powers of the heavens will shine sevenfold forever" (Enoch 91:16).

The teaching is carried one step further in the two New Testament passages. Peter writes that the renovation is to be preceded by a cosmic conflagration in which the heavens will be dissolved and the elements will melt with fire (II Peter 3:13). In Revelation the new creation sets the stage for the descent of the new Jerusalem in which God will dwell with man in the absence of sorrow, death, and pain (Rev. 21:1).

The crucial question is whether the "earth" in this series of passages refers to literal ground or is part of a description of the eternal state in the only terminology available to the biblical writers. Those who understand it in the first sense (actual earth) normally take the Isaiah passage as a description of the coming millennium. The obvious problem here is that Revelation indicates that this "renovation" (chapter 21) *follows* both the millennium and the final judgment. The editors of the Scofield Reference Bible resort to a bit of *Ubereinstimmungforschungen* (roughly translated, "Make it harmonize!") at this point saying, "Verse 17 looks beyond the kingdom-age to the new heavens and the new earth, but verses 18–25 describe the kingdom-age itself."

It seems more plausible that we are dealing with a typical example of the limitations of finite speech faced with the problem of giving expression to that which belongs to the category of the infinite. "New heavens and a new earth" is not a reference to some future universe which is to replace the present one. It is born out of the necessity to speak meaningfully about a future bliss for which the existing cosmos must step aside. In short, it speaks of eternity in the language of time; of a dimension of reality which resists being accommodated to our space-time structure.

Do you think that hell is a place or a condition?

A quick answer would be, both. Jesus said it would be better to enter life with one eye than to be thrown into the "hell of fire" with two (Matt. 18:9). In Revelation 1:18 the glorified Christ identifies Himself as the one who has "the keys of Death and Hades." Both verses understand hell as a place. Yet it is not the geographical location of hell that is significant. In the New Testament its connotations are damnation, sorrow, and torment. There men weep and wail and gnash their teeth (Matt. 8:12; 13:42; 22:13; 24:51; 25:30). The disciples are warned to fear the one who can destroy both body and soul in hell (Matt. 10:28). The rich man of Luke 16:19-31 was in torment in the flames of Hades.

The most common New Testament word for hell is Gehenna. This ravine to the south of Jerusalem where the smoke of burning refuse constantly arose lent itself as a figure of punishment in the next life. Hades was the underworld or realm of the dead. In Revelation 20:14 Hades, along with Death, is thrown into the lake of fire. II Peter 2:4 speaks of the angels who sinned as having been cast by God into Tartarus (the deepest abyss of Hades and a place of punishment).

While the New Testament never speaks of hell as a condition of life rather than a place of future punishment, the actual location is beyond our knowledge and is of no significance in comparison with the state or condition that exists for those who, by refusing the gift of God's love, assign themselves to everlasting punishment. Although the doctrine of hell is offensive to some, it exists as one of the basic teachings of the New Testament. Those who hold the Scriptures in high esteem accept it as true and are eternally grateful to God for providing forgiveness of sins which leads to the presence of God rather than His absence.

Why does the Bible teach rewards? I'll be satisfied just getting into heaven.

You are right in holding that the Bible teaches a doctrine of rewards. For example, I Corinthians 3:14, "If the work which any man has built on the foundation survives, he will receive a reward."

However the Bible does not teach a *quid pro quo* morality in which good behavior is bribed by the promise of reward. C. S. Lewis has pointed out that proper rewards are not tacked on to the activity for which they are given but are the activity itself in consummation (cf. his sermon, "Weight of Glory"). For example, a happy marriage, not money, is the natural reward for love. Victory, not advance in rank, is the proper reward for a battle well fought. In each case the reward is germane to the activity itself.

What then is the "reward" offered to the Christian who bends every effort to a life of holiness and service to God and man? Certainly not a string of merit badges which in heaven will distinguish him from those mediocre souls who barely made it. His reward will be a greater capacity to know and enjoy forever God's presence.

Will we know our loved ones in heaven?

While there is no specific verse which says unequivocably "You, John, will know Mary," the overwhelming implication of related scriptural teaching is that the fellowship begun this side of heaven will not be cancelled when we enter into that perfect and eternal fellowship.

On the mount of transfiguration Peter apparently recognized Moses and Elijah (Matt. 17:4). The rich man in Hades saw Lazarus in the bosom of Abraham (Luke 16:23). Jesus in His resurrection body was recognized by Mary (John 20:16), the disciples (John 20:20), and others (I Cor. 15:6-8). From what the Bible teaches about life beyond the grave it would seem to me that the burden of proof lies upon those who feel that God must cancel all the deep relationships of life as a prerequisite for joy in heaven.

I have never been able to make heads or tails out of the Book of Revelation. Can you recommend a good commentary?

Before we talk about commentaries let me suggest you try a fairly simple experiment. Take a modern speech New Testament, get comfortable someplace in the house where you can't see or hear the television or won't have to answer the telephone, then read the Book of Revelation in a leisurely fashion from start to finish without worrying about what any particular verse might mean. If you do this prayerfully and carefully, you will most likely learn more about the central message of the book than you would from attending a prophetic conference or reading a commentary.

How could this be? There are several basic reasons. One is that commentaries by their very nature deal primarily with a multitude of specific details. Exactly who are the two witnesses? What about the locusts with women's hair and tails like scorpions? This is what they are supposed to do: they *comment* on the text; they do not replace it.

The problem is that detailed attention to incidentals shifts the impact of the book away from its central message. A good commentary should prepare the reader to return to the biblical book itself and experience more fully what it has to say to him.

Another reason why commentaries on Revelation are less illuminating than the book itself is that they inevitably tend to force a larger interpretive pattern onto the book. Most of the basic questions seem to have been settled ahead of time and the role of the commentator is to demonstrate how all the individual verses support this predetermined thesis. It is interesting to note how writers in the opening chapters use such qualifying phrases as "it seems to me" or "it is probably true," but by the time they arrive at the last chapters have so convinced themselves that they are emboldened to say, "there is no doubt that" or "it has been established that" in reference to passages equally ambiguous as those in chapter one!

Revelation is a distinctive literary genre in the New Testament. Although prophetic it comes in the imagery and thought forms of apocalyptic. The one great question which determines how each writer handles Revelation is, How is this language to be understood? A commentary on Acts, for example, does not face the same question. "They weighed anchor and sailed along Crete, close inshore" (Acts 27:13b) means exactly what it says.

If this statement were found in Revelation, however, the various schools of interpretation would understand it differently. The preterist would take it as a first-century statement about an ocean voyage. The historicist would find its fulfillment in some event in history (perhaps the Spanish Armada in maneuvers prior to its assault on England in the late sixteenth century). The futurists would project it ahead in time and ask whether or not the church was on board, especially since the ship is about ready to go into a storm (the tribulation?). The symbolist would discover the timeless truth that when the anchor of faith is hoisted, not even staying close to the island of organized religion will prevent disaster!

While a basic approach has to be established for consistent exegesis, that approach ought not to be a definitive theology but a careful understanding of the nature of the literary genre in which the book is written. Once this has been established, let the book say whatever it wants to, even if it runs counter to our pat eschatological theories.

But what about commentaries? If you are a careful student of Greek, my suggestion is I. T. Beckwith, *The Apocalypse of John* (Baker, 1967). It has been around quite a while (since

1919) but I know of no better treatment of the text. For the average layman who wants a historical premillennial presentation, read George E. Ladd, *Commentary on the Revelation of John* (Eerdmans, 1972). John F. Walvoord, *The Revelation of Jesus Christ* (Moody, 1966) is a reasonable presentation of the dispensational point of view. The most popular of the amillennial commentaries is William Hendriksen, *More Than Conquerors* (Baker, 1939). George B. Caird, *The Revelation of St. John the Divine* (Harper and Row, 1966) will give the average evangelical a number of theological jolts but also some profound insights.

My own somewhat technical commentary, "The Book of Revelation,"belongs to the *New International Commentary on the New Testament* set (Eerdmans, 1977). I have recently completed a layman's commentary and the study guide on Revelation to be released in paperback by David C. Cook (*What Are We Waiting For?*) in 1979.

But remember, after reading the commentaries, go back to the book! The sovereignty of God and the ultimate overthrow of evil resound throughout the book and will make your heart sing for joy as you realize once again that the death of the Lamb leads directly to the countless multitudes around the heavenly throne praising God forever.